Global Issues and Comparative Education

Global Issues and Comparative Education

Series Editor: John Sharp

Editors: Wendy Bignold
and Liz Gayton

LearningMatters

First published in 2009 by Learning Matters Ltd

British Library Cataloguing in Publication Data

A CIP record for this book is available from the British Library.

ISBN: 978 1 84445 208 8

Cover design by Topics – The Creative Partnership
Text design by Code 5 Designs
Project Management by Swales & Willis Ltd, Exeter, Devon
Typeset by Kelly Gray
Printed and bound in Great Britain by TJ International Ltd, Padstow, Cornwall

Learning Matters Ltd
33 Southernhay East
Exeter EX1 1NX
Tel: 01392 215560
info@learningmatters.co.uk
www.learningmatters.co.uk

FSC
Mixed Sources
Product group from well-managed
forests and other controlled sources

Cert no. SGS-COC-2482
www.fsc.org
© 1996 Forest Stewardship Council

Contents

Editors   vi

Contributors   vii

Acknowledgements   viii

Introduction   1
Wendy Bignold and Liz Gayton

1   What is comparative education?   4
Jean Clarkson

2   Back to the future of early childhood: same but different   18
Patricia Giardiello and Joanne McNulty

3   Primary practices and curriculum comparisons   32
Jackie Barbera and Deirdre Hewitt

4   High schools and high stakes assessments   48
Anthony Edwards

5   Money and massification: international issues in higher education   64
Wendy Bignold and Liz Gayton

6   Teacher education in a changing context   80
David Cumberland, Wendy Bignold and Bart McGettrick

7   Education and social care: friends or foes?   94
Sue Kay-Flowers

8   Education for citizenship: different dimensions   109
Phil Bamber

Index   124

Editors

Wendy Bignold is Vice Dean of Education at Liverpool Hope University and Co-Director of the Institute for Research in Education and Society at St Xavier's College, Mumbai, India.

Liz Gayton recently completed her term of office as Dean of Education at Liverpool Hope University.

Contributors

All of the contributors are members of the Education Deanery at Liverpool Hope University.

Phil Bamber has worked extensively on teaching projects in Asia. His research interests are in-service learning and global citizenship.

Jackie Barbera is a senior lecturer in education and has extensive experience of working in primary education.

Jean Clarkson is a senior lecturer and has co-ordinated International exchange for 12 years. She is presently co-ordinating the MA Education. Her research interests are student retention and international education.

David Cumberland is Vice Dean of Education at Liverpool Hope University, having previously spent over 20 years in Primary and Secondary education as a teacher and local authority adviser.

Anthony Edwards has wide experience of working in schools and universities in the UK and abroad. His research interests include creativity and new technology in learning and teaching.

Patricia Giardiello is a senior lecturer in education with a background embedded in early childhood education primarily as a teacher both in Italy and the UK. Her research interests include young children's participatory rights.

Deirdre Hewitt is a senior lecturer. She teaches on Childhood and Youth Studies Course as well as being a co-ordinator for Primary English. Her research interests are in early reading and the effect of illiteracy on youth crime.

Sue Kay-Flowers is a senior lecturer in Childhood and Youth Studies and has wide experience of social work with children and families. Her research interests include cross-cultural work and children's rights and participation.

Bart McGettrick is Dean of Education at Liverpool Hope. He is Professor Emeritus of Education at the University of Glasgow and a regent of Bethlehem University, Palestine.

Joanne McNulty is a senior lecturer in education with experience of teaching at Foundation Stage and Key Stage 1. Her research interests are learning in early childhood.

Acknowledgements

In this book we have been helped by educators in the countries we have written about and particularly wish to thank:

Chrissie D'Costa, St Xavier's College, Mumbai, India

Drs Barbara and Richard Mezeske, Hope College, Michigan, USA

Dr Rajendre Shinde, St Xavier's College, Mumbai, India

Feng Frank Su, Liverpool Hope University, Liverpool, UK

Introduction

Wendy Bignold and Liz Gayton

In an increasingly globalised world any serious student of education has to pay attention to international perspectives. This study of different countries can be considered to be 'Comparative Education'. Comparative education is the comparison of education systems, processes and outcomes both in different countries and within a single country. Education is not simple but a hugely complex concept, a highly significant activity and a constantly debated topic within families, local communities, regional societies, national governments and international organisations. Education is something we have all experienced, either formally, in a school or other structured setting, or informally, within our home. As such, we all have a view on what constitutes 'good' education or effective teaching or what the curriculum should include and how pupils and students are best assessed. Our experiences are individual to us and are profoundly influenced by our personal backgrounds, be it our mother-tongue language, economic income or political philosophy. This is true for both individuals and for countries. A country's political system will influence its education system; for example, a strong dictatorship may introduce a monocultural national curriculum so ensuring that alternative styles of government or political views are not taught in schools. A multicultural nation, on the other hand, may adopt a system of schooling which allows parents considerable choice in their children's education; for example, in the faith or language of instruction.

This book introduces you to the study of comparative education, by exploring what it is and what value it can hold for students of education and future educators such as yourselves as well as policy makers. It provides you with strategies and guidance on making your own comparisons of different countries, while exploring a number of examples. In doing so, it gives you both skills and knowledge necessary for this exciting area of educational study and research. Comparative education, as has already been hinted at, is both a simple idea and a hugely complex undertaking. This should not put you off, of course, but encourage you to explore it, read about it and *do it* for yourself. The complexity comes in the comparison of different education systems. How can you compare two different countries, with different cultures, different levels of national resources, different structures of government and different aims for their education systems? Can you compare them? Can you compare them fairly? The answer to these questions must be a resounding 'Yes!', but it requires critical thinking, sensitive reflection and objective analysis. It also requires knowledge and understanding of the countries you are interested in, of their different cultures and, perhaps most importantly, of your own education system and your own cultural background so that you can recognise your own biases and prejudices. In looking at other education systems you will learn more about your own country and often more about yourself and in particular the varied influences that have helped to make you who you are today.

As a student of education or its related disciplines, such as early childhood studies or social care, you may find yourself in a position to help shape other people's lives, particularly the lives of children and young people. This is an exciting role to take on, but one which brings with it huge responsibility. In such a role, an enhanced understanding of yourself, the society in which you live and work, and the place of education within it is essential. This book will take you on a journey of investigation and understanding of the education system in England

and draws on other countries within the UK. Comparisons with other countries, including Italy, Romania, Poland, India and America, will help you to explore different educational issues at the beginning of the twenty-first century in our increasingly globalised world.

Governments around the world are more and more interested in examining education systems in other countries, to assess the success of those systems and determine which, if any, aspects can be utilised in their own countries to benefit themselves and their citizens. This is recognised by international organisations who can assist them and you in making comparisons, by publishing relevant data and information:

Governments are paying increasing attention to international comparison as they search for effective policies that enhance individuals' social and economic prospects, provide incentives for greater efficiency in schooling, and help to mobilise resources to meet rising demands.

OECD, 2007, page 3

The following chapters will introduce you to some ideas and reflections so that you may undertake comparisons across countries. Illustrations relating to certain themes, such as compulsory school-starting age or funding of higher education, will provide a theoretical basis for you to develop your own interests. Books on comparative education tend to adopt one of two approaches to make comparisons manageable. They compare countries either by regions, comparing the Pacific Rim countries of Malaysia, Singapore and Thailand for example, or they compare phases of education, such as secondary education, in different countries. This text takes the second approach which draws on the specific expertise of different authors, all of whom have been professional educators and are now academics, researching and teaching in the broad field of education. To a large extent the countries discussed in this book have been chosen because of the authors' first-hand experience of their education systems and they often draw on personal experiences to illustrate their writing. In that sense it is eclectic and alive, rather than traditional and systematic.

Chapter One is an exploration of comparative education providing a historical overview of the discipline and discussing why it is increasingly important. It raises some of the issues in undertaking comparisons across countries and cultures. It suggests both quantitative and qualitative sources and methods which you might find useful if you want to compare different education systems yourself.

Chapter Two initiates the book's examination of different phases of education by starting at the beginning as it explores early years education. It discusses the key stakeholders in preschool education and care: children, educators and parents. It emphasises the importance of play, considering its place in early learning in the UK, Italy and New Zealand.

Chapter Three moves the focus to a comparison of primary education, recognised by the United Nations as a universal right of all children. It explores starting ages of schooling, the statutory curriculum for primary children, types of assessment used and other key themes in this age phase by looking at the examples of England and Romania.

Chapter Four continues to develop the pupil age profile by investigating secondary or high school provision. It adopts a more quantitative approach than most other chapters by including comparative statistics on the performance of children in English, mathematics and science from different countries using internationally recognised assessment tools. It does this with particular reference to England and Finland.

Chapter Five is the last one to follow the development of pupil age as it explores issues in higher education with adult learners, whether coming directly from school or as mature students. It compares the approach taken by Britain, India, China and America to current issues faced by universities and colleges of higher education, such as expansion of student numbers and the maintenance or enhancement of quality, and related issues.

Chapter Six presents a comparison of teacher education, a key element in any education system as it provides much of the necessary workforce. It explores, in particular, government influence over initial and continuing professional development using England and Poland as examples. It also touches on recent developments in the training and education of other educators and related professionals.

Chapter Seven presents a reflection of recent global trends in education at the start of the twenty-first century. In particular it explores the integration of education and social care which is taking place in many countries keenly watched by others round the world. England and Romania are looked at closely in this context.

Finally, Chapter Eight seeks to remind you that comparative education takes place in a context of increasing globalisation. National governments are no longer educating pupils just to be effective citizens of their country but to be effective global citizens. It compares strategies adopted by England, America and India for global citizenship education and considers its place in the curriculum.

No book on comparative education can compare all aspects of education in all countries. With this in mind we have sought to introduce you to some key themes in Comparative Education through examples with which we are familiar. In keeping with other books in this series we have included a variety of tasks (practical, critical thinking and reflective tasks) which are intended to help you reflect on what you read here. Figure icons within the task boxes indicate whether the task is designed as a group or individual project. We also include some recommended reading and references that help you to develop and enhance your knowledge and understanding. This will support you in analysing critically the information with which you are presented and in sourcing additional information. Most importantly though, it will help you to develop the skills and understanding necessary to make your own comparison of countries in which you are particularly interested. Perhaps you have been assigned a country to research as part of an assessment task, or you have visited a country which has led to an ongoing interest in it, or you may have personal links to a particular country. Whatever the reason for your interest, this text will enable you to develop that interest academically by researching its education system and comparing it with others. The development of the internet and other worldwide media has ensured that we are all global citizens. We all need to be able to look outside our immediate environment to understand other countries and cultures. As current educators and as future educators we have a particular responsibility to foster the education of global citizens. The study of comparative education provides a strong theoretical and empirical base for questioning conventional beliefs about the role of education in society and how best it can be developed to enhance intercultural harmony.

Chapter 1

What is comparative education?
Jean Clarkson

Learning outcomes

By the end of this chapter you should be able to:

- understand what comparative education is and what value it has for educationalists, both practitioners and policy makers;
- understand how to make comparisons of educational systems, philosophies and practices and appreciate how these are influenced by your own cultural background, values and attitudes;
- have a good understanding of the challenges and cautions associated with the study of comparative education;
- find sources of data gathered on the systems of education both in the UK and overseas;
- apply the principles of two approaches to carrying out your own qualitative research into comparative education.

Chapter outline

This chapter outlines the focus and purposes of comparative education suggesting who might be interested in making comparisons and how rigorous comparisons are made both quantitatively, through national and international surveys, and through qualitative methods of data collection, observations and talking with people. It presents an historical overview of the development of comparative education accounting for the reasons that most countries want a dynamic educational system to serve the ever-changing demands of this modern global society. A number of quantitative surveys are presented and two models commonly used for qualitative investigation into a country's education system and related issues are proposed.

As well as knowledge and understanding of other education systems students of education need the fundamental skills and ability to research and understand other cultures. This helps them to understand how and why these have evolved and to develop a tolerance and respect for different systems and customs. Comparative education is that strand of the theory of education which is concerned with the analysis and interpretation of educational practices and policies in different countries and cultures. A curiosity about other cultures and an understanding of the relationship between wider society and education practice underpin an understanding of diversity and internationalism, crucial for the global society in which we live (Alexander, 2001). Globalisation has increased the requirement for those in the education professions to understand that many countries are interdependent, economically, technologically, politically and ecologically, and thus we need a deep understanding of how we all inculcate the next generation and educate them for the future we face as global citizens.

Our appreciation of the strengths and weaknesses of our own educational system are enhanced when we have a sound understanding of systems in other nations. Knowledge of the social milieu, cultures, customs, political and economic processes of others allows us to put our own systems into context. An understanding of other education systems can help us make comparisons with our own. This, of course, means that we have to be open to other cultures; we have to recognise and put aside our prejudices and focus instead on objective and robust comparative information in order to make informed and meaningful judgements and choices.

Cultural identity

We all have a cultural identity and shared outlook which provides us with a sense of 'belonging'. This belonging may be to a small group, such as a university sports team or a large group, such as a nation or religion. Within those groups we have shared pre-judices, about other teams, other nations and other religions. A confrontation or even an interaction with another group, or culture, can be threatening because it implies a difference of opinion with different answers to fundamental questions of why we live the way we do. *Culture shock* is a phrase used to describe our reaction when we encounter behaviour that we would not necessarily consider appropriate even if it is the norm in another culture. A common reaction to different cultures is fear, which can lead to distrust and hostility.

The starting point for comparisons of educational systems is the rigorous collection of information, both qualitative and quantitative, about issues such as:

- the nature of the curriculum;
- accountability and cost effectiveness;
- administrative practices, retention and attrition;
- achievement and national standards;
- children at risk;
- decentralisation and teacher autonomy;
- equality of opportunity, inclusion and multiculturalism;
- education and training of educational professionals.

The data collected from such sources provides objective evidence to support or refute views and enable unprejudiced conclusions to be reached. From this data you can then delve further into case studies of individuals. This type of analysis helps educationalists to consider the implications of doing things differently, remembering that any educational system is set within the historic, social, economic and political context of the country concerned. As students of comparative education it is good to discuss differences rather than to say that one system is *better* than another, as such a view may be largely objective. Some students from England, for example, are surprised that not all children are taught a national curriculum and that there are considerable differences in other countries on issues such as when children are taught to read. It is important to consider the historical evolution of the educational system of the country under investigation, as well as how influences such as racial and national prejudices have intervened to create the current curriculum.

Reflective Task

Recognising your own cultural identity

Read the following information and, in the context of your own educational experience, answer the questions at the end:

Broadfoot (2003) reminds us that

in studying foreign systems of education we should not forget that the things outside the school matter even more than the things in the school and govern and interpret things inside.

Broadfoot, 2003, page 275

Broadfoot is referring to the culture of the community or country in which the school is located. This deeply influences what goes on inside the school, such as the subjects that are taught and the values that are encouraged. An example might be the sports that are taught and played in PE. Traditionally in the UK these have included football for boys and netball for girls, based on cultural significance attached to different sports and cultural expectations of what is appropriate for different genders.

Reflect back on your own schooling:

1 How would you describe the culture of the local community in which you lived and went to school?
2 How would you describe the wider culture of the country in which you grew up?
3 How might these cultures have influenced your education? Try to give some specific examples.

Interpreting from our own experiences

To a large extent we take the educational system in which we grew up for granted. We have inherited a national and even local system of education which has been developed over many years primarily as a result of the actions of politicians, religious leaders and parents. Decisions about what is taught and the pedagogy used to teach are preceded by socially induced perceptions. To understand how culture changes over time just compare the values and attitudes held by you and your peers with those of your grandparents. If this comparison is extended to other countries then it would seem to be very unlikely that one can successfully superimpose the systems of one country on to another. Nevertheless, serious objective investigation of an area across several countries with all their evident advantages and disadvantages is beneficial for critical reflection and the initiation of change.

Even when adaptation and adoption is impossible, an understanding of how other systems work has value. Through comparisons we have a better understanding of what *we* do and we learn that some of our practices are not based on reason and experience but on a reverence for tradition and prejudice. We have inherited educational systems which are the outcome of a long series of decisions and habits that are accepted rather than examined. They are more social and governmental than strictly educational (King, 1979; McLean, 1995).

The study of comparative education allows us to challenge present systems by re-interpretations of what is feasible or desirable. Comparisons with other educational systems will allow you to observe through a different lens and interpret the findings giving a new perception. This is an interpretivist model based on our own unique experiences and creates insider research. Popper (1963) called this *subjective knowledge*. It is the world of our conscious experiences and we interpret further experience within this context. That is why it is useful. If we have an open mind, and do not cling unthinkingly to traditional ways, our consideration of alternatives prevents education from remaining static.

Historical overview of international perspectives

The discipline of comparative education has existed for hundreds of years. The early foundations have been described as *travellers' tales* because they presented random observations of how children were educated (Trethewey, 1976). Ancient Greeks and Romans admired the discipline of Spartan education and Plato explained how some Spartan institutions could be adapted to the needs of his own city of Athens. The Italians of the early medieval period were intrigued by the tales brought back by Marco Polo of how the Chinese taught their children (Crossley and Watson, 2003). Jean-Jacques Rousseau offered suggestions for educational reform to Poland in the 1700s demonstrating further an early interest in other educational systems across countries.

When formal schooling was established in Britain in the nineteenth century, educators went abroad to examine the systems in other countries to discover practices that might profitably be adopted at home. Matthew Arnold, an interpreter of high culture and an inspector of schools, travelled to Europe at the request of the Royal Commission in 1859. His reports included sweeping comparisons such as *French walls are barer than ours*, *the reading and writing are better than ours* and *arithmetic is more intelligently taught*. His comments were general and he made subjective interpretations of what he observed, apparently without the authority of evidence (McLean, 1995), something which would be discouraged now as we put an emphasis on data and evidence to enable us to draw informed conclusions.

A more contemporary example of comparative education influencing policy in the UK can be seen in the introduction of secondary comprehensive schooling in the 1960s and 1970s. During World War One, 1914–18, men of all ranks and social classes fought side by side in the British army. As a result of this, after the war equality of opportunity was considered a vital development in modern society and particularly education. This view continued after World War Two and there was a great deal of optimism that the power of education could be used to create a better and more economically successful world. Plans were made by many countries for large-scale expansion of education. Many European leaders looked to educational practices overseas for innovative methods that might improve literacy and numeracy in particular. The UK looked towards the USA for an alternative model and saw high schools where children of all abilities learned together. At that time England had a tripartite system of grammar schools, secondary modern schools and technical schools for children of three different 'ability' levels; they were segregated into this system at the age of eleven. While allocation of pupils to schools was based, theoretically, on ability, this system largely reinforced class divisions. As a result of studying the system in the USA, the tripartite structure was changed to the comprehensive system in the UK in the latter part of the twentieth century (Alexander, 2001). In Scotland there was a system of senior secondary and junior secondary schools to which children were allocated based on ability. In 1967 these were largely replaced with comprehensive schools. The independent schools remained largely aloof from these changes.

More recently, policy makers in England have examined the successful Pacific Rim countries, such as Japan and Korea, and Scandinavian countries, such as Finland and Sweden, in the light of their apparent 'superior performance' in international surveys of educational achievement. As a result of this comparative analysis, policies such as the National Literacy and Numeracy

Strategies were devised for every child in England (Reynolds and Farrell, 1996). Perhaps as a consequence of this interest the International Baccalaureate has emerged as a significant element in English education. In Scotland and Northern Ireland the curriculum is not designed in the same ways and so curricula are different and relate to the needs of those countries.

Why is research into comparative education increasingly important?

The onset of the technological age of information means that the world, including the world of education, is contracting. One major rationale for comparative studies is to improve our competency and not limit our knowledge and experience to that which we already know or do not know. We attempt to push the boundaries further and extend our education practice out of our comfort zone. It takes courage to do this and there is often a resistance as we move away from that with which we are familiar. Indeed we may fear the realms of the unknown and what is outside our knowledge. Without drawing on the collective wisdom from educationalists in other countries, issues such as curriculum change, assessment strategies and pedagogical research may be more difficult to understand. Without listening to the experiences of our colleagues, both at home and abroad, teaching may be static and our professional practices stagnant and myopic (Mazurek and Winzer, 2006). New knowledge is created as insights are made through the observation of other ways of educating. Insights are created through investigating a different slant on issues and the realisation that there can be a different way to do things.

Transposing one entire educational system onto another is never an option, but as we study it we see ways of taking parts of a system that will improve our own and of assimilating it into our own organisation. All education is dynamic and the systems and structures roll on. Replacing a system with something *different* but not necessarily *better* is a real danger; that is where the skill of the educationalist emerges as they make decisions, based on evidence, about what can be transferred to improve learning. Crossley and Watson (2003) call this being a part of the *intelligentsia*; educationalists are expected to take a leading role in social debates, be they political, economic or cultural. This is done from a position of knowledge and understanding about how the wider world of education functions in different countries around the globe and taking the best ideas to improve your own system.

A further aim of comparative education is to offer short cuts to avoid some of the grave mistakes that were made by educational systems that have since changed. A practical, student-focused example of this is corporal punishment for children. This was a feature of education in the UK in the nineteenth and, in some cases, the first half of the twentieth century. This is now considered unacceptable and has in fact been banned by the European Court of Human Rights. Some countries, however, still maintain corporal punishment and overseas education students studying in the UK who spend time in schools may have to investigate alternative behaviour management strategies to corporal punishment. On return to their own country they will then be in a position to offer alternative forms of behaviour management that respects children's rights.

In the twenty-first century we have sophisticated global citizens who are competent to deal with the rapidly changing world and uncertain realities. Understanding issues beyond our own experiences and perspectives enables us to make informed choices appropriate for the future. Stavenhagen (2008, page 162) draws attention to the task of education today in the globalised world. He says: *In today's interconnected world, living together peacefully has become a moral, social and political imperative on which depends to a great extent the survival of humankind.* Education in its widest sense is called on to play a major role in this shared, worldwide task.

The internationally respected United Nations Educational Scientific and Cultural Organisation (UNESCO, 1995) urges higher education institutions to teach students to become well-informed and motivated citizens who can think critically, analyse the problems of society, consider and apply solutions to them and, in doing so accept social responsibility. Comparative education courses in universities and colleges allow students to widen their vision of the world from what is perceived as acceptable and the norm, to encompass and consider alternative world views.

How do we ensure comparisons are rigorous?

Research in comparative education and international interest in large-scale comparative studies of educational achievement and the methodologies employed in their design is often motivated by the concern for improvement in performance, notably revealed in league tables:

Intensified global economic and educational competition has helped to heighten the prominence of comparative and international education – and involved a wider range of stakeholders in both the research process and the interpretation of the findings.

Crossley and Watson, 2003, page 56

Policy makers, funders and consumers of education are increasingly looking abroad as they seek ways of dealing with the implications of league tables, market forces and the demand for more cost-effective education.

To compare two or more systems of education can be vague and driven by hunches and prejudices. Matthew Arnold, referred to earlier, made sweeping statements on the standards of arithmetic teaching in France in the 1850s and then, apparently randomly, moved on to comment on the walls of the classroom. This is not the role of comparative education, although hunches may influence what we study. The first stage is to decide on the areas to be compared. To compare fairly and with precision and attention to detail, research methods have to be meticulously planned from the outset. Time spent at the planning stage reaps dividends later.

International agencies and databases

Quantitative methods of research can produce objective, factual and measurable data. Such methods appear in the media through international surveys and there are many organisations that collect information and statistics from schools throughout the world using instruments such as questionnaires and surveys. Some of the largest research centres and data collection programmes include those listed below. They all have their own websites which can easily be found via search engines:

- The Institute of Education Science at the US Department of Education National Centre for Education Statistics provides educational statistics on many different countries. One influential piece of research is the *Trends in International Mathematics and Science Study* (TIMSS). This provides reliable and contemporary data on the mathematics and science achievement of students from many countries.
- The Progress International Reading Literacy Study (PIRLS) is an international comparative study of the reading literacy of young students. PIRLS studies the reading achievement, behaviours and attitudes of fourth-grade students in the United States and students in the equivalent of fourth grade in other participating countries. PIRLS was first administered in 2001 and included 35 countries, and was administered again in 2006 to students in 45 education systems. The next PIRLS is scheduled for 2011.

- The Programme for International Student Assessment (PISA) is a system of international assessments that focuses on 15-year-olds' capabilities in reading literacy, mathematics literacy and science literacy. PISA also includes measures of general or cross-curricular competencies such as learning strategies. It is organised by the Organisation for Economic Co-operation and Development (OECD), an intergovernmental organisation of industrialised countries. Begun in 2000, PISA is administered every three years.
- The Department for Children, Families and Society (DCSF) in England publishes a database of statistical information from the UK. This website contains details of all research projects funded by the DCSF and the Department for Innovation, Universities and Skills (DIUS), as well as those projects previously undertaken by the Department for Education and Skills (DfES) which the two new Departments have replaced. This seems entirely concerned with the UK only.
- The UNESCO Institute for National Statistics based in Canada provides statistics on many countries and their educational systems. This association reports on issues such as the strong effect of social inequality on primary education systems in many countries and the challenge to provide all children with equal learning opportunities.
- The UNESCO Centre for Comparative Education Research (UCCER) is a well-established research centre at the School of Education, University of Nottingham. UCCER has attracted major funding for its projects, with the key focus of its research being the comparative study of education policy and practice in the context of international development.
- The Organisation for Economic Co-operation and Development (OECD) was established in 1961 in Paris and has a membership of 30 countries. It publishes 250 new titles per year, written in English and French. The OECD includes a Centre for Educational Research and Innovation (CERI). The OECD considers that both individuals and countries benefit from education. For individuals, the potential benefits lie in general quality of life and in the economic returns of sustained, satisfying employment. For countries, the potential benefits lie in economic growth and the development of shared values that underpin social cohesion. Education systems must constantly reinvent themselves to remain relevant and to take advantage of innovative approaches and new technologies.

All these agencies and databases can be used to analyse two or more countries and the existing quantifiable data collected by these organisations can be used as a context for further research and a springboard for personalised research. Be careful! Statistics require some healthy scepticism as they seldom tell the full story and can be interpreted in many ways.

Practical Task

Using international surveys

Each group member should choose a different survey or organisation listed in the previous section, for example PISA or OECD. Each person should search the internet to find the home page of their survey or organisation. From the home page make a note of:

- the aims of the survey or organisation;
- its scope – how many countries does it involve?;
- the frequency of its output – how often does it publish data?

As a group compare your findings. The information you share will help you all to know which survey or organisation to consult when you need particular data. Consider together:

- Which surveys or organisations do you think will be most useful to you as students of comparative education? Why?
- Do you think this would differ for educators and other professionals or for policy makers? Why might this be?
- Are there any listed in the earlier section that you would not consider using? Why?

Local research

There are many more local agencies engaged in research and data collection, including much smaller-scale investigations. This research is often specific and rigorous, based on collected evidence and recorded data. Information might be gathered through interviews, observations, field notes and policy documents. Much qualitative research has been undertaken in the study of comparative education. A seminal text which is an excellent example of qualitative comparisons is *Culture and pedagogy: International comparisons in primary education* (Alexander, 2006).

When making educational comparisons across countries it is not necessary to collect all the data yourselves. It is perfectly valid to analyse existing data and put your own interpretation on any outcome. Often your interpretations will be grounded in qualitative comparisons. One challenge is to devise ways of examining issues first hand while in the country of scrutiny, through interviews, observations and questionnaires. This requires a more personal approach and seeks a deeper relationship with the person or country from whom you are seeking information, but when done rigorously and systematically, provides useful and valid information. The key is always critical analysis.

There are several models which can be used for systematically and qualitatively examining the educational system of a country and collecting data. Two that students find most useful are the Didactic Triangle, and The Ideological Cross.

Both approaches can be used as tools to help you reflect critically on the educational system of a country in a systematic way (Morrison and Ridley, 1989). The following explanations are designed to help you use these models. It is helpful to be able to consider different countries within each model as a means of carrying out comparative education.

The Ideological Cross

The Ideological Cross establishes two intersecting lines to describe the major characteristics of a country's society and its education system. When using this model you begin by looking at the criteria in each box (see Figure 1.1). Using these criteria you consider the extent to which the society in the country being focused on is open or closed, and the extent to which the education system is child-centred or teacher-centred. You then place the country on each of the two axes (for example, if you think it is more closed than open put your mark nearer the 'closed' box). This enables you to consider the relationship between the two placings and so the ideological influences on education by society. If you repeated this approach with a different country, its position on the grid mighty provide a good start in analysing the relationship between different societies and their education systems.

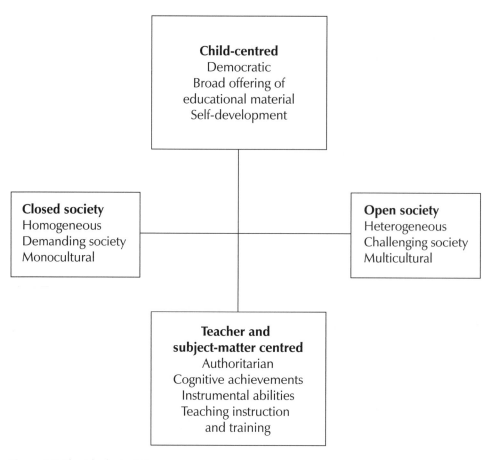

Figure 1.1 The Ideological Cross

The Didactic Triangle

The Didactic Triangle takes as its starting point the learning and teaching process, comprising *knowledge* which is passed between the *learner* and the *teacher* (see Figure 1.2). Thus the content or curriculum, the learner and the teacher form the three points of the triangle. This model presents an opportunity to observe the process of education from the point of view of learning and teaching. Learning and teaching are at the heart of education and a study of the dimensions will provide insights into how a specific educational system works and the philosophies it embraces. It facilitates investigation of further questions such as 'What is the role of central government in prescribing the content of the curriculum?' Sometimes the triangle is placed inside a circle to indicate that teaching and learning always takes place in a context.

You can use the triangle for different levels of analysis. Some use it simply to distinguish between the three points. Others take it further to look at relationships between the three components. Some take it further still to consider how the three components fit together to create an integrated whole, the education system.

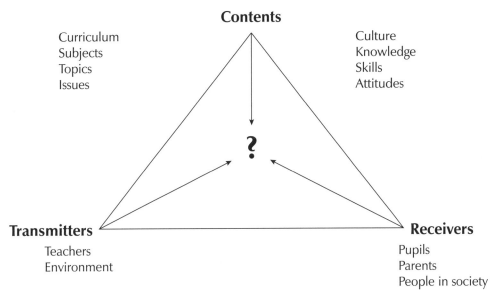

Figure 1.2 The Didactic Triangle

Critical Thinking Task

The Didactic Triangle

For this exercise, focus on the education system in which you were educated as it is the one you are likely to know most about. Draw the triangle on a large sheet of paper.

Firstly list the major areas of CONTENT at the top point.

- What subjects did you study at school? Include any choices you could make.
- Were there any issues in school that might have been dealt with through school parliaments and/or discipline panels? What about homework? How old were you when homework began, and how long did it take?
- If your education was in England, did all the children in your school cover the National Curriculum? Were you put into groups covering different things according to difficulty level (differentiated)?
- Knowledge is learning facts. Give some examples of the knowledge you gained at school.
- Skills are learning how to do things. Give some examples of the skills you gained at school.
- Attitudes are qualities like perseverance, positivity and enthusiasm. How were these attitudes taught in your school? What were the underlying feelings you had about walking into school? Delve back into your memory and describe how you felt.

Secondly, list the key TRANSMITTERS by the left point.

- Consider the role of your teacher. Did they always transmit knowledge to the pupils? How many times did *pupils* present knowledge to the rest of the class?
- How did the teachers know what to teach?
- What other professionals worked in your school? Were there teaching assistants or learning mentors? What did they do?

Thirdly, list the main RECEIVERS by the right point of the triangle.

- Pupils are mainly the receivers of education but was there any opportunity for the community to come into school to learn?
- Did parents have any instruction about, for instance, listening to reading?
- Would you have liked more say as to what you learned?

When you have done this consider the relationships between the three aspects of the triangle. Would you say your system of education was more or less subject-centred, teacher-centred or pupil-centred?

You might like to consider the same education system against the Ideological Cross.

Challenges in comparative education

When examining new and different education systems it can be easy to get overenthusiastic about them. It is particularly important, therefore, to gather information that is accurate and reliable and not just based on prejudicial beliefs. This is critical if interpretations and comparisons are to have any validity. The source of the information should be reliable and authentic.

Accuracy and reliability. There can be a problem of bias when one has a vested interest, if it is your own country you are investigating, for example. You may have nationalistic feelings which you need to identify and acknowledge. Some international studies such as one commissioned by DfID (Department for International Development) have been criticised for being biased and using Northern Hemisphere research methods (Hoppers, 2001). It has been alleged that when a government presents information for national surveys such as TIMMS or PISA, its determination to present its nation in the best possible light may lead to falsification of educational statistics, or alternatively to present information that is based on a particular favourable analysis. Analysing the source of information critically is therefore always essential.

Comparability. You cannot compare apples with pears. As you may be working in different languages the interpretation of words establishing comparability is central. A series of essential questions will guard against the lack of comparability. Do identical terms carry the same meaning? There is a tendency to assume that meanings attached to particular terms in your home setting are the same as elsewhere. However, this is frequently not the case, for example, 'public school' in the USA means state school, but it means private school in England. As this demonstrates, every country has a different range of meanings for educational terms (Corner and Grant, 2004). Are the same groups being compared? Are all abilities represented in the tests used in the survey or are some of the low achievers taken out of the test so that the percentages of achievement in one country goes up? Differences in purpose not only present difficulties in comparing types of school but also in examining quite different assumptions in societies which have different bases for education. Examining schools in a cultural context will avoid rash comparisons that fail to take account of the different purposes schools are expected to serve in different countries.

It is important to consider carefully the choice of systems in countries or cases for comparison. If the purpose of comparison is policy making then it may be more effective to choose 'referenced' countries, or those with whom our own society is linked by tradition of development. For example, in this context it may not be reasonable to compare education in the UK with that of a developing country.

Generality–specificity trap. The criteria by which material relevant to an area of study are selected will be specific and these should be balanced with acknowledgement of general trends and movements in the bigger picture. When this does not happen, people use overgeneralised phrases like '*All* English primary schools' or the 'US state education'. It is important to be cautious, and to always keep the context in mind.

The future of comparative education

The early developments and insights of comparative education reveal our curiosity about what happens in different parts of the world, and has deep roots. Human beings from different countries talk about differences in all social situations and young people seem willing to change their assumptions and consider differences rather than to stand firmly against change. Cultural borrowing will help decision makers adopt different practices and seek to transplant models of good practice in, for example, school improvement, achievement, teaching and learning from one system to another (Alexander, 2001).

Studying the theory and reading about international trends can be very informative but does not compare to actually experiencing differences in education first-hand. Gap years, exchange programmes and study-abroad initiatives have provided huge opportunities for students to experience other educational systems and educational transformation. Exchange students, for example, experience another educational culture first-hand and are often surprised that their own educational systems do not prevail in all countries – they are then able to consider an alternative system. Yet such opportunities seem to be waning in the economic climate of the twenty-first century. Undoubtedly though, the future of educational comparison will be influenced by the development and proliferation of the internet greatly expanding access to information. The forces of globalisation have increased interest in international trends in education among policy makers, practitioners and theorists; as such the discipline of comparative education has a strong future.

Chapter Summary

Comparative education is concerned with breaking with our prejudices and considering other education systems in a meticulous and rigorous way. This has to be done within an informed context.

- Mere hunches and guesswork are not reliable means of comparison, as each country has a legacy of culture shaped by unique traditions and customs.
- The professional, political and moral decisions of any country are linked to their interaction with the global society.
- One system of education cannot be taken from one country and superimposed on the system in another country, as that system has evolved within the prevailing political, economic and cultural context of its original country.
- No matter how effective a system might appear to be, only aspects of it can be adopted and assimilated.
- Education is undoubtedly an agent for change in all countries and there should be an ongoing debate about what aspects of education create the 'perfect society'.

The world is becoming increasingly interdependent – economically, politically and technologically. In addition, a deep understanding of each other's systems of educating our young people creates informed global citizens. In a world under threat from conflict and hostility, the study of comparative education provides hope for the future.

Research focus

Task 1

This chapter has made reference to a seminal book on comparative education and research:

- Crossley, M and Watson, K (2003) *Comparative and international research in education.* London: Routledge.

Reading the book will help you develop your knowledge and understanding of comparative education. The second chapter ('Multidisciplinarity and diversity in comparative and international education') gives a detailed account of what comparative education is. It provides an extension to this chapter and is particularly recommended to you. What do Crossley and Watson say we can learn from comparing the education process of different countries?

- Crossley and Watson also give some interesting historical examples of how educational procedures were spread worldwide. Make notes on one that interests you.

Task 2

Read the chapter by Power and Whitty, 'Devolution and choice in three countries', in G. Whitty (2002) *Making sense of educational policy.* Power and Whitty undertake a comparative study of compulsory education in England and Wales, America and New Zealand. They explore, specifically, recent developments in the education systems in these three regions which have increased school autonomy and parental choice. Read the chapter and make notes, not on the content, but on the process of comparison.

- How do the authors compare the countries?
- What background information do they give, if any, on each country?
- How do they deal with any cultural or contextual differences?
- Do they actually compare like with like?
- Do they make judgements? If so what are they based on?
- In your opinion are they fair judgements?
- What have you learnt from the chapter about undertaking comparative education?

References

Alexander, R (2001) *Culture and pedagogy: International comparisons in primary education.* Oxford: Blackwell Publishing.

Alexander, R (2006) *Culture and pedagogy: International comparisons in primary education.* Oxford: Blackwell.

Broadfoot, P (2003) Editorial: Post-comparative education. *Comparative Education,* 39(3): 275–8.

Corner, T and Grant, N (2004) Comparing educational systems, in Matheson, D (ed.). *An introduction to the study of education.* London: David Fulton.

Crossley, M and Watson, K (2003) *Comparative and international research in education: Globalisation, context and differences.* London: RoutledgeFalmer.

Hoppers, W (2001) About how to reach the truth in development co-operation, ODA/DfID education papers. *International Journal of Educational Development,* 21(5): 463–470.

King, E J (1979) *Other schools and ours.* London: Holt, Rinehart and Winston.

McLean, M (1995) *Educational traditions compared.* London: David Fulton Publishers.

Mazurek, K and Winzer, M (2006) *Schooling round the world.* New York: Pearson.

Morrison, K and Ridley, K (1989) Ideological contexts for curriculum planning, in Preedy, M (ed.). *Approaches to curriculum management.* Milton Keynes: Open University Press.

Popper, K (1963) *Conjectures and refutations: The growth of scientific knowledge.* London: Routledge and Kegan Paul.

Power, S and Whitty, G (2002) 'Devolution and choice in three countries' in Whitty, G (ed.) (2002) *Making sense of educational policy.* London: Paul Chapman.

Reynolds, D and Farrell, S (1996) *Worlds apart? A review of international surveys of educational achievement including England.* London: HMSO.

Stavenhagen, R (2008) Building intercultural citizenship through education: A human rights approach. *European Journal of Education*, 43(2):161–179.

Trethewey, A R (1976) *Introducing comparative education.* New York: Pergamon.

UNESCO (1995) Article 9 UNESCO World Conference. Available at **portal.unesco.org/education/en/ev.php-URL_ID=7152&URL_DO=DO_TOPIC&URL_SECTION=201.html** (accessed 30 April 2009).

Chapter 2

Back to the future of early childhood: same but different

Patricia Giardiello and Joanne McNulty

Learning outcomes

By the end of this chapter you should be able to:

- critically review early childhood education using historical, cultural and philosophical perspectives;
- appreciate the importance of experience in the early years of life;
- understand why it is important for the early years educator to work in partnership with parents;
- compare and contrast common threads of Early Childhood Education and Care in England, Italy (Reggio Emilia) and New Zealand (Te Whariki).

Chapter outline

This chapter focuses on the way in which Early Childhood Education and Care plays a significant part in ensuring young children are given the best start in life. It begins by considering early childhood education from historical perspectives and introduces the work and philosophies of key early years pioneers, such as Froebel, Montessori and Steiner.

Common threads in varying early years programmes in England will be identified and comparisons drawn with the Reggio Emilia and Te Whariki approaches, from Italy and New Zealand, which have attracted worldwide attention. It concludes by reflecting on how early childhood education must respect each child as an individual with the right to be heard and listened to.

What is Early Childhood Education and Care?

A young child starts learning prior to birth, and certainly long before he or she attends a school or even a pre-school setting. This means that the role played by parents and carers is fundamental to healthy development. The education and care of young children are inextricably linked and inseparable.

'Early Childhood Education and Care' is a term that is used by governments and international organisations, such as the Organisation for Economic Co-operation and Development (OECD), because it captures succinctly the different national systems of both education and care from birth to six years, or eight years in certain countries. Nurseries, kindergarten, day care, day nurseries, children's centres and playgroups are all settings which are considered under this term.

The Government paper, *Every Child Matters: Change for Children*, was published in England in 2004. This nationwide agenda encapsulated the total integration of education and care throughout the country, emphasising not only learning but also the holistic well-being of children and young people as the context for learning. To this end, the framework for *Every Child Matters* is underpinned by five outcomes:

- be healthy;
- stay safe;
- enjoy and achieve;
- make a positive contribution, and;
- achieve economic well-being.

Central to the *Every Child Matters* policy is the recognition of the responsibility that schools, early years settings, hospitals, social services, police and other services have towards the educational achievement and well-being of children. Radical and constant reorganisation is ongoing to ensure full integration of children's services and a 'joined-up' approach to governance, planning and provision of support.

Historical and philosophical perspectives: early childhood philosophers

The long tradition of Early Childhood Education and Care in the West began mainly in response to the industrial revolution of the early nineteenth century when families moved away from the home and community into factories and cities. Perhaps the most renowned of the early pioneers who worked to protect young children and their families was Robert Owen (1771–1858). A mill owner and social reformer, he established the first community nursery school where care, education and health were provided, in New Lanark in Scotland in 1816. Although a philanthropist, he recognised that caring for his workforce and their families led to increased productivity and he saw how important the early childhood years were in dealing with the new social order of the time. In 1910, Margaret and Rachel McMillan developed nursery education in Deptford, an area of extreme poverty, in the east end of London. They too placed an emphasis on children's health which became central to their philosophy of a broad and humane education establishing the traditions of nursery education and day care in the UK, America and other countries (Nurse, 2007). At about the same time, the philosophies and ideas of Pestalozzi, Froebel, Steiner and Montessori really started to influence the knowledge and understanding of educationalists across the world about young children's development.

Pestalozzi (1746–1827), a Swiss early years teacher, recognised the individuality of young children and argued that they should be free to pursue their own interests and draw their own conclusions about the world they were experiencing. In this they should be supported by teachers who were skilled in developing, rather than implanting, knowledge (Darling, 1994).

The German teacher, Friedrich Froebel (1782–1852), was the first philosopher and educator to advocate that play encouraged young children to learn, by allowing them to explore their environment both indoors and outdoors. We see his legacy today in effective early childhood education where play and positive relationships between children and adults is at the centre of learning.

Maria Montessori (1870–1952), renowned as being the first woman physician in Italy, founded the Montessori Method of education in 1907. She designed a 'prepared environment' in which children could freely choose from a number of developmentally appropriate, didactic activities and practical life experiences such as dusting, sweeping, polishing shoes and setting the table. Play was viewed as the work of childhood and a child's freedom to choose underpinned the development of autonomous learning. Montessori's legacy was a method of education which combines a practical approach based on a carefully planned learning environment with a philosophy centred on the idea of freedom for the child. She saw children as intrinsically motivated to learn and who could absorb knowledge without effort when provided with the right kind of activities at the right time in their development. Montessori referred to these as *sensitive periods*. Through careful observation the *direttrice* (as Montessori called her teachers) directed the child towards learning opportunities.

Rudolph Steiner (1861–1925) was born in what is now Croatia. He believed that education should help children to fulfil their full potential but he did not believe in pushing them towards goals that adults, or society in general, believed to be desirable. The first Steiner school opened in Germany in 1919. The curriculum is based on a flexible set of pedagogical (teaching) guidelines, founded on Steiner's principles that take account of the whole child. It gives equal attention to the physical, emotional, intellectual, cultural and spiritual needs of each pupil and is designed to work in harmony with the different phases of the child's development. Steiner also considered the environment as important; classrooms are painted in warm colours with an abundance of soft, natural materials and wooden equipment which are incorporated into the children's play. The main focus in a Steiner kindergarten is developing physical and language skills in a stress-free environment in preparation for formal schooling. As in Montessori settings, children carry out practical tasks which reflect home life but resources are multipurpose to encourage children's play and imagination. A good relationship with parents and other adults is at the heart of the Steiner approach which sees the kindergarten as a home from home. Steiner's legacy to early childhood education is his emphasis on developing the imagination through creative play experiences but within clear structures and routines.

It is interesting to note the development of early years education and care taking place in a number of countries, at similar times with pioneers of various nationalities. Undoubtedly they would have been interested in each other's philosophies and practices and this is an example of early comparative education.

Nearly two centuries after Pestalozzi was studying children, his child-centred philosophy can be seen in both Te Whariki and the Reggio Emilia approach. To some extent the Reggio Emilia approach is also rooted in Montessori philosophies. Both share a constructivist approach to learning; children learn by interacting with the environment and the people around them. Both approaches believe children are active in their own learning and that the environment is vital in stimulating exploration and learning. In both, the role of the teacher is to act as a guide to help in new discoveries. Montessori really has had a worldwide influence and it is not uncommon to see kindergartens in many countries using some of her methods.

Reggio Emilia

In Italy, the prosperous city of Reggio Emilia has become famous worldwide for its progressive kindergartens and early years centres. The former Communist Party which has run the area since World War Two remains firmly in charge, but under a new name, the Party of the Democratic Left. Because of the political philosophy underpinning Reggio Emilia's services within a framework of social justice, the child is seen as the *subject of rights* (Malaguzzi, 1997, page 19). The Reggio Emilia approach to Early Childhood Education and Care was founded on a strong relationship with parents. It was established from the vision the parents had for their children after their experiences of living through a fascist, tightly controlled regime under Mussolini. This vision emerged from the value that parents placed on educating children as true citizens in a democratic society. Therefore, parents today still see it as their right and responsibility to actively contribute to their children's learning.

Te Whariki

In New Zealand the range of services in Early Childhood Education and Care is diverse, but all are connected by the Te Whariki curriculum which was introduced in 1996 as a result of 'Pathways to the Future', the ten-year strategic plan developed by the Early Childhood Education and Care sector and the Ministry of Education. Prior to the development of the Te Whariki curriculum, many parents, and mothers in particular, set up their own play centres in their communities. Pramling-Samuelson, Sheridan and Williams (2006) comment that as these developed the parents became more involved and received training with some going on to become supervisors and qualified Early Childhood Education and Care teachers. Today, in some Early Childhood Education and Care settings (for example Playcentres) the parents and whänau are directly responsible for the education and care of the children (whänau is a Mäori word, meaning extended family.) In other settings (for example education and care centres) paid staff are responsible. The importance of this relationship with parents is reflected in all the principles of Te Whariki, and specifically family and community (New Zealand Ministry of Education, 1996). The objectives and practices of early childhood education in New Zealand are based on key guiding principles, one of which is to work in partnership with parents/whänau to promote and extend the learning and development of each child who attends or receives the service (New Zealand Ministry of Education, 1998, page 6, cited in Pramling-Samuelson *et al.*, 2006). 'Pathways to the Future' acknowledged that the links between the wide range of Early Childhood Education and Care services are not always strong, however, and that greater collaboration between services is required in order to improve outcomes and provide better opportunities for children and their parents.

The best start in life

The increasing recognition of the importance of Early Childhood Education and Care has been articulated by UNICEF, the United Nations Children's Fund (previously known as the United Nations International Children's Emergency Fund):

Every child must be ensured the best start in life – their future, and indeed the future of their communities, nations and the whole world depends on it.

UNICEF, 2008

Throughout the world this has resulted in a significant expansion of Early Childhood Education and Care provision. In the UK, early childhood education is at the forefront of political agendas and educational research. With this expansion there has been a global trend by academics and practitioners to define the effectiveness and quality of provision. Within the context of greater public accountability governments are also attempting to establish whether high-quality early childhood services are providing 'value for money'.

Time spent in early childhood settings is an extremely important period in young children's lives wherever in the world this might be. In 2004 the UK Government set out its ten-year strategy to improve national childcare (HM Treasury, 2004). Its vision was *to ensure that every child gets the best start in life and to give parents more choice about how to balance work and family life* (page 7) and it had quality as a key theme. A recent study by the Daycare Trust (2007) reviewed and analysed existing research and UK government statistics. They concluded that availability of quality Early Childhood Education and Care provision for children and their families throughout the country was highly variable, despite the commitment to quality made by the government three years earlier. The report asserts that the root of this lack of consistency is grounded in the tension between cost and quality. Because of the market-led mixed economy approach to funding in England (an economy guided by investors and entrepreneurs rather than controlled by government) there are concerns about the sustainability and lack of real investment such as that found in Scandinavian countries, where their respective governments have opted for heavily subsidised systems of funding. The report suggests that investment is essential if the UK government's aim, to improve outcomes for every child and reduce the gap between the most disadvantaged children and their peers, is to be successful.

In an ideal world, in order to ensure that government-funded initiatives are successful, they are often underpinned by research findings to ensure they are properly tested before implementation. For example, research, such as the *Effective Provision for Pre-School Education (EPPE) Project* (Sylva *et al.*, 2004) shows that attendance at early childhood settings of high quality has an unquestioned impact on children's learning and development. However, defining and researching 'quality' is not simple as it is a value-laden term and judgements can never be value free, not least because we are all from different cultural and social groups and consequently have different ideas about what we expect from Early Childhood Education and Care. Nevertheless, the research findings from the EPPE project are extremely valuable to early years staff and parents wishing to explore the implications of interpreting effective practice and provision according to different ideas about quality. In summary, children were found to make better all-round progress (Sylva *et al.*, 2004) in settings where:

- staff used open-ended questioning and encouraged 'sustained shared thinking';
- differentiated learning opportunities were provided to meet the needs of individuals and groups, such as bilingual, special needs, girls/ boys etc.;
- a balance was achieved between staff-supported, freely chosen play, and staff-led small group activities;
- settings viewed educational and social development as complementary;
- staff had a good understanding of appropriate pedagogical content;
- staff supported children in being assertive while at the same time rationalising and talking through their conflicts;
- there was strong parental involvement, especially in terms of shared educational aims;
- a trained teacher acted as manager and a good proportion of the staff were qualified early years practitioners to graduate level;
- there was strong leadership and relatively low staff turnover.

Recent scientific research on brain development which shows the importance of experiences in a child's early years has also influenced an understanding of 'quality'. The rapid development of brain cells in infancy and the remarkable learning that takes place as a result of developing connections in the brain underline just how crucially important the early years are (Blakemore and Frith, 2005). Recent neurological research with brain-imaging technology has shown that babies and young children who experience an interactive and stimulating environment develop cognitively at a faster rate. This observation lends support to the benefit of the work of Pestalozzi, Froebel, Montessori and Steiner, who all advocated experiential learning (i.e. having real life problems to solve).

Reflective Task

Effective Provision for Pre-School Education (EPPE)

Longitudinal studies such as EPPE have a direct impact on government initiatives and policies and therefore it is vital that those involved in working with young children and their families take these findings into consideration in relation to practice and provision.

With this in mind, complete one or more of the following exercises to further develop your understanding of effective early childhood and care.

- Select two or three summary statements from the earlier list of EPPE project findings. Consider the implications, opportunities and challenges for both staff and parents in ensuring shared educational aims for young children.
- Review an early childhood policy document with which you may be familiar, for example the Sure Start *Code of Practice* (2006). To what extent has the impact of the EPPE project findings been made explicit or implicit in the document?
- Visit the EPPE website at **eppe.ioe.ac.uk**. Use the information there to reflect on ways in which the research findings have impacted on early years policy and provision described in this chapter or that you have observed in an early years setting.

Partnership with parents

The importance of working in partnership with parents for the benefit of the child has long been acknowledged as a key aspect in determining the quality and effectiveness of Early Childhood Education and Care. Research shows that partnership between parents and professionals enhances the experiences of young children. A study investigating the effects of the Peers Early Education Partnership intervention programme found that working directly with parents enhanced the cognitive and social-emotional development of young children. The EPPE project (2004) found that children made better progress in settings where parental involvement was valued. It concluded that *what parents do* (with their children) *is more important than who parents are* (Sylva et al., 2004, page ii). However, despite the wealth of research which highlights the value of partnership there is also considerable evidence to suggest that the development and maintenance of the partnership can be problematic (Hughes and McNaughton, 2001). According to Paige-Smith (2004) the role of parents in their child's education has moved away from the idea that they are there to support the educator, who was the expert, to the idea that it is the parent's right to be involved in every aspect of their child's learning. If an effective partnership is established then there will be many positive outcomes for all concerned.

Support for parental partnership comes from a range of historical, political and cultural sources. Partnership with parents is an area which was acknowledged as being important in Early Childhood Education and Care since Froebel, who believed that the education of a child began at birth and that parents and teachers alike supported children in their learning. Later, Montessori felt that a synchronisation must exist between home and school in order for the child's experience to be balanced and uncomplicated. Montessori felt the role of the mother was particularly important.

Political support for parental partnership

In 1967, the UK government commissioned the *Plowden Report* which identified the need for schools in the UK to establish partnerships with parents and for parents to be given more information in relation to their child's progress. Since then there has been a succession of government reports or acts focusing on or referring to the early years. These include:

- *The Children Act*, 1989, which saw a move away from children being seen as passive recipients of adult care and control to them being seen as individuals to whom their parents had responsibility.
- *The Education Reform Act* of 1988 which gave parents further opportunity to be listened to, for example, through their entitlement to sit on school governing bodies and therefore having opportunities to voice their opinions on important matters relating to the education of their children.
- The *Start Right* report of 1994 viewed parents as their children's first educators. This report identified three areas of need in relation to parents: the introduction of paid parental leave, provision of care for pre-school children of employed parents and high quality education for all children over three years of age.
- *The Scottish Schools (Parental Involvement) Act* was passed in 2006 by the Scottish Parliament. It set out to ensure parents are fully involved with their child's education and learning. Parents are encouraged to be active participants in the life of the school. In addition to the research discussed above which demonstrates that parental partnership in the early years has positive effects, why else might governments want to promote it?

With the introduction of *Every Child Matters* early years education and care is experiencing more collaboration and partnership with parents than ever before. Sure Start, for example, is a government-funded programme which works to bring together education, care, health and family support services relevant to the lives of young children and their parents. Partnership with parents is not specific to the UK but is gaining popularity in other countries and is well established in some, such as Italy, in the Reggio Emilia approach to early years, and in New Zealand in the Te Whariki curriculum.

Reflective Task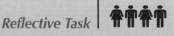

Challenges to partnership

Read the case study below and then answer the questions:

Hayley has 18-month-old twins and two other children aged three and five years. Hayley takes her children to school every day but often doesn't arrive until just before school begins as she lives some distance away and does not have access to her own transport. Hayley prefers to wait at the school gate with her children until the bell goes as she finds it awkward getting in and out of the gate with her double-buggy. Hayley does not speak with her children's teachers often although she met the nursery teacher once when a home visit was made just before her three-year-old started nursery. She has attended one parents' evening for her eldest child. Both children bring home regular news letters so Hayley and her partner are able to keep up to date with what their children are doing. Hayley attends an evening class in music at the local college, so twice a week at home time she collects the children and drops them off at their grandparents' house where they stay until their dad collects them at 6pm.

- What factors could be inhibiting Hayley from taking a more active role in the partnership?
- Could the school do anything to improve the partnership for parents like Hayley? What might this be?

The early years curriculum

Even before devolution was established in 1997, shifting power from central government to regional control, England, Northern Ireland, Scotland and Wales each had its own system of Early Childhood Education and Care. A common thread, however, is that each country in the UK acknowledges the importance of appropriate provision for young children. In the UK, this has led to the development of a number of appropriate curriculum models over recent years. Perhaps it is worth noting, at this point, that Rinaldi (2006) considers the term 'curriculum' unsuitable for representing the complex and multiple strategies that are necessary for sustaining children's knowledge-building processes. She believes that learning does not proceed in a linear way but rather is constructed through *contemporaneous advances, standstills and retreats that take many directions*. Pramling-Samuelsson et al. (2006) display similar beliefs and describe the curriculum as a framework, guidelines, a text guiding the direction of work in Early Childhood Education and Care and not as a narrow way of prescribing a set sequence of educational activities. Only through a secure theoretical knowledge base of how young children learn and develop could this shared understanding come about. Yet within this shared understanding there are slight variations.

In England, the Early Years Foundation Stage, or EYFS as it is commonly known, is a statutory framework for all settings providing for children from birth to 5. The EYFS brings together the principled approaches of *Birth to Three Matters* and the *Curriculum Guidance for the Foundation Stage* and also includes aspects of *the National Standards for Under 8s Day Care and Childminding*. In Scotland there is a similar system but there remains a separate phase for birth to 3. There is currently a phase 3 to 5 but this is under a national review, with a new 3 to 18 *Curriculum for Excellence* soon to replace existing provision. In Wales, the *Foundation Phase* provides for children from 3 to 7. Currently, the draft *Framework for Children's Learning in the Foundation Phase* is being trialed as part of a pilot project in 41 settings between 2004 and 2008. In Northern Ireland the *Enriched Curriculum* project resulted in the establishment of the *Foundation Stage* in 2007 for children in their first two years of primary school. Therefore, provision for young children in the UK is similar in that each constituent country has, and continues to develop, curricula which provide common philosophies and goals for all educators to build on.

Oberhuemer (2005) indicates that there are varying reasons that underpin the increasing interest in curricula for Early Childhood Education and Care. One reason offered is that newly emerging *knowledge societies* are endeavouring to make early years settings visible. Although the term has been around since the 1960s, in present times the concept of the knowledge society has become an essential framework of reflection for not only countries of the OECD, but also for emerging economies and developing countries. According to the United Nations Education, Scientific and Cultural Organisation, *a knowledge society is a society that is nurtured by its diversity and its capacities* (UNESCO, 2005, page 17). The very idea of a knowledge society emerges from a learning society and owes much to current research and innovation. According to Oberhuemer (2005), another reason for exploring national and international curricula that, ideally, early years professionals should have a curriculum guide which provides:

- a shared framework;
- mandatory guidelines which are also seen as a quality improvement and equality measure;
- a common framework for enhancing communication between staff and parents.

The importance placed on having a shared framework stems from the fear that in the past early childhood education was underfunded and undervalued and that if a unified front is not presented then public support would diminish (Isenberg and Jalongo, 2003). Within the global dimension of a unified front it is important to consider the diverse cultural experiences of children in each country, and whether or not it is possible to share the same framework or guidelines.

A principled approach to the curriculum

Although differing perhaps in title/name and age phase all provision in the UK is based on the solid foundations of long established and ever present principles of Early Childhood Education and Care. What is common amongst provision in the UK are clear themes of inclusion, uniqueness, relationships, self-esteem, the value of play, holistic development and the importance of the child at the heart of everything that happens.

In Italy, the Reggio Emilia approach is based on a clear set of guiding principles which stem from the image of a child as a competent learner from birth with both democratic and human rights. Furthermore, a child we might refer to in the UK as a child with special needs, is in Reggio Emilia settings a child with special rights. As a reaction against people who classify the Reggio Emilia Approach as working with an emergent curriculum, Rinaldi (2006, page 205) suggests that in order to be understood by those who believe in the importance of a pre-determined curriculum it is useful to develop the idea of a contextual curriculum. Referred to as *Progettazione* it stems from the children's own interpretations which give meaning to the world around them, their contexts, and capacity to build theories with an appreciation that other minds can share their own values and beliefs. In this process of joint investigation both teachers and children document their own daily activities and learning using symbolic processes.

The Te Whariki curriculum of New Zealand bases its approach on many of the same principles but also includes a strong emphasis on promoting the attitudes and customs of two cultures (biculturalism), children's rights and on developing dispositions to learning. The Te Whariki curriculum is described by the New Zealand Ministry of Education as *the sum total of the experiences, activities and events, whether direct or indirect, which occur within an environment designed to foster children's learning and development* (1996, page 10). *Te Whariki* is Maori for, and uses the metaphor of, a woven mat. This is based on the Maori ideology that everything is interconnected and learning takes place in the social world as put forward by the social constructivist Vygotsky and described in Pramling-Samuelson *et al.* (2006). It is a socio-cultural approach that endeavours to meet the needs of children from diverse social and cultural backgrounds. Te Whariki highlights a set of goals for children to achieve but these focus more on developing the child as a competent and confident learner rather than being a set of specific performance-related skills.

The need for knowledgeable educators

Unless we know and understand our children, unless we act effectively on what we know, we cannot help them very much.

Bruce, 1997, page v

In Early Childhood Education and Care today, there is an increasing range of professionals who work with young children such as the qualified teacher, the early years professional, the childminder, the children's centre manager and others who are part of the team around the child. This can also include speech therapists, educational psychologists and social workers. All play a vital role in supporting the child in their earliest years and therefore they have a responsibility to maintain and continually develop a comprehensive understanding of Early Childhood Education and Care.

In the more distant past, key philosophers and theorists, such as those introduced earlier, acknowledged the importance of well-qualified adults in the field of early childhood education. Margaret McMillan established one of the first training schools for early years teachers in 1930. Here, students took a three-year full-time course leading to a Froebel certificate. Unfortunately, this recognition of the need for qualified educators did not continue for a number of decades and it has only been in more recent times that the demand for qualifications has increased.

The need for well-qualified educators is a key finding of the Effective Provision for Pre School Education research (Sylva *et al.*, 2004) introduced earlier. In terms of the effects of quality and specific practices in pre-school this research found that in settings that have staff with higher qualifications children make more progress. Indicators of quality include having a trained teacher as manager and a good proportion of trained teachers on the staff. This is also linked to better outcomes in pre-reading and social development. The report found that in effective settings staff:

- encourage episodes of *sustained shared thinking* (when two or more individuals work together in an intellectual way to solve a problem, for example);
- have a good balance between child-initiated and adult-led interactions;
- have a good grasp of the appropriate pedagogy for a child's understanding to develop.

As a result of these findings two of the research recommendations are to ensure staff have both curriculum knowledge and knowledge and understanding of child development and that the content of both initial and continuing professional development course should be improved.

In recent years, government policy has led to the development of nationally recognised degree courses for educators in early childhood. Central government's ten-year Childcare Strategy for England, launched in 1998, has also acknowledged the importance of well-qualified knowledgeable adults which has led to an increase in demand for such courses. Further to this in England the Children's Workforce Development Council established the Early Years Professional Status. The Early Years Professional (EYP) is responsible for leading practice and ensuring quality in the setting. The government has made it clear that its aim is to have an EYP in every full day care setting by 2015 and one in every children's centre by 2010.

In the Reggio Emilia approach the *pedagogista* (early years practitioner) must acknowledge and support what the children themselves perceive as relevant to them. The skill of the Reggio Emilia educator is not to take a curriculum and relate it to the individual child, but to listen to, learn with and respect the child and their role in their own learning so that the child is truly free to follow their own interests, in their own time and at their own level. Reggio Emilia educators are co-researchers with children and see themselves as theory builders as well as theory consumers. They use practice to create theory through the ongoing process of posing hypotheses and gathering empirical data through careful observation, documentation and interpretation of the children's learning and development. This is in contrast to most co-operative learning approaches, where the role of the adult is usually seen as that of facilitator. As Rinaldi (2006, page 125) states:

The learning process is certainly individual, but because the reasons, explanations, interpretations and meanings of others are indispensable for our knowledge, it is also a process of relations – a social construction . . . the teacher is not removed from her role as an adult but instead revises it in an attempt to become co creator, rather than merely a transmitter of knowledge and culture.

As in England, New Zealand's Strategic Plan for Early Childhood Education states that all early childhood teachers in teacher-led services are to be fully or provisionally registered by 2012. This means that by 2012 all teachers must have had three years of training and a year of supervised practice. In Te Whariki the adult has a similar role, in that the process of learning begins with the child and the adult must gain insights into the way the child learns and what motivates him or her to learn. This is where the metaphor of the woven mat can be used again and although there is a curriculum model in this approach it is designed so that the curriculum can be woven into the individual experience of the child. This curriculum can be described as a 'spider's web' model rather than the 'step' model (Penn, 2000) which might describe England's Early Years Foundation Stage where children develop through a series of stages in order to meet the Early Learning Goals. The 'spider's web' model relates to the way the principles, strands and goals of Te Whariki provide a framework that *weaves through the process of talk, reflection, planning, evaluation, and assessment* (May and Carr, 2000, page 156), and emphasises a model of knowledge and understanding that grows through increasing complexity and richness.

A similarity between Reggio Emilia and Te Whariki is the idea of documenting or narrating the children's learning. The process of documentation in the Reggio Emilia Approach also recognises the importance of recording the child's learning experience in terms of what they are doing, feeling and thinking (OECD, 2004). A Reggio teacher will document not only the process the child has gone through but also their own observations that they have made over the period of time the project has taken to complete. This documentation, because it combines words, images, photographs and so on, allows children to see and remember what they have done, gives the teacher an insight into the learning that has taken place and acts as a form of communication with the parents (OECD, 2004).

In Te Whariki these are known as Learning Stories and developed as part of the work of Margaret Carr; here they form part of the assessment process. They differ from conventional observation records in that they describe what the child is feeling and doing and focus on dispositions for learning. Learning Stories are linked to socio-cultural learning theory since they involve the interaction of context, location and people. They are used by teachers to document the child's engagement with their learning, to plan for further learning and to share with the child's family, thus acknowledging the importance of relationships in the child's learning.

Critical Thinking Task

Comparing early years provision

This chapter has explored differing perspectives on Early Childhood Education and Care. A number of common threads have been identified but it is clear that within these commonalities lie differences.

Dividing into groups, preferably in pairs, choose one of the countries referred to in this chapter and using the factors listed below, think critically about why your chosen country's approach to Early Childhood Education and Care may not be easily translated to another country.

- cultural
- historical
- economic
- societal
- political

Discuss your conclusions with your partner.

Suggest possible ways in which the perceived barriers may be overcome to facilitate the translation of Early Childhood Education and Care from one country to another.

The rights of the young child

During the International Year of the Child, 1979, the Polish Government proposed a convention for children's rights. Following a lengthy re-drafting of the Polish proposal the final version was given approval by the United Nations General Assembly in 1989 and became known as the United Nations Convention on the Rights of the Child. In November 2005 the UNCRC released its *General Comment No. 7, Implementing child rights in early childhood* which emphasises that young children's rights to express their views and feelings should be recognised in *the development of policies and services, including research and consultation.* MacNaughton *et al.* (2007) identify two recent developments emerging from the *General Comment No. 7* (page 163) which are particularly significant to the early years:

the appearance in the international early childhood literature of a new model of young children as 'social actors' and the increasing interest by government agencies in several countries in creating and sustaining child centred policies and practices.

Both Te Whariki and Reggio Emilia provide strong examples within their frameworks of social justice that see the child as the subject of rights. The Reggio Emilia approach has developed distinct sociological and pedagogical features over the years which now see the child as a *citizen of rights.* Putting the child at the centre of the provision is an acknowledgement of the importance of that child and his or her early experiences. That the child is now seen as an active participant in the setting is an acknowledgement of the rights of the child.

Chapter Summary

This chapter has presented early childhood practice in three countries, England, Italy and New Zealand. Each of these countries has a child-centred curriculum, planned by appropriately trained and educated professionals and underpinned by partnership with parents.

- The importance of giving young children the best start in life has been a key theme of this chapter.
- Positive early learning experiences help children to develop their self-esteem and self-image, to begin to understand their world and to interact positively with those around them.
- Citizenship is a key theme in education today and the foundation for it is led in the early years.
- As national governments are striving to improve or enhance their education systems, to ensure they are fit for the twenty-first century, many of them are choosing to invest in quality early years provision, as described here.

Good quality Early Childhood Education and Care is underpinned by the rights of the child and the parents to high quality early learning and care but also recognises the importance it can make in developing effective citizens.

Research focus

Task 1

Iram Siraj-Blatchford is a prominent early years writer and advocate in the UK. Read her chapter (Quality Teaching in the Early Years) in Anning, Cullen and Fleer, *Early Childhood Education: Society and culture* (2004). Here she discusses the nature of provision and argues the case for the importance of the adult's role in teaching as well as their role in facilitating opportunities for learning. Identify the different models of Early Childhood Education and Care she presents and consider how the adult's role varies in each. Apply this to what you now know about Early Childhood Education and Care in England, Italy and New Zealand.

Task 2

A further reference which focuses on the role of the adult is an article by Rose Davies who identifies the key competencies and attributes of a teacher of young children. Although this article discusses these from a teaching perspective it is an interesting read for anyone with an interest in working with young children. See 'Making a difference in children's lives: The story of Nancy, a novice early years teacher in a Jamaican primary school' (Davies 2008).

Read the article carefully and make notes on what it tells you about early years philosophy in Jamaica. Which of the approaches written about in this chapter does Jamaica most relate to for early years education and care? Try to find evidence in this chapter to support this additional reading.

References

Blakemore, A and Frith, U (2005) *The learning brain.* Oxford: Blackwell Publications.

Bruce, T (1997) Early childhood education (2nd edn). London: Hodder and Stoughton Education.

Darling, J (1994) *Child-centred education and its critics*. London: Paul Chapman.

Davies, R (2008) Making a difference in children's lives: The story of Nancy, a novice early years teacher in a Jamaican primary school. *International Journal of Early Years Education* 16, 1: 3–16.

Daycare Trust: National Centre for Social Research (2007) *Childcare nation?* London: Nuffield Foundation Publication.

HM Treasury (2004) *The National Childcare Strategy.* London: The Stationery Office.

Hughes, P and MacNaughton, G (2001) Building equitable staff-parent communication in Early Childhood settings: An Australian case study. *Early Childhood Research and Practice*, 3, 2:(online). Available at **http://ecrp.uiuc.edu/v3n2/hughes.html** (accessed 1 May 2009).

Isenberg, J P and Jalongo, M P (eds) (2003) *Major trends and issues in Early Childhood education.* New York: Teacher College Press.

MacNaughton, G, Hughes, P and Smith, K (2007) Early childhood professionals and children's rights: Tensions and possibilities around the United Nations General Comment No. 7 on Children's Rights. *International Journal of Early Years Education*, 15, 2: 161–170.

Malaguzzi, L (1997) History and cultural notes on the Reggio Emilia experience, in Filippini, T and Vecchi, V (eds) *The Hundred Languages of Children: Narrative of the Possible.* Reggio Emilia, Italy: Reggio Children Inc (19–21).

May, H and Carr, M (2000) Te Whariki: Curriculum voices, in Penn, H (ed.) *Early childhood services: Theory, policy and practice.* Philadelphia, PA: Open University Press.

New Zealand Ministry of Education (1996) *Te Whariki Early Childhood Curriculum.* Wellington: Learning Media.

Nurse, A D (ed.) (2007) *The new Early Years professional.* Abingdon: Routledge.

Oberhuemer, P (2005) *International Perspectives on Early Childhood Curricular.* International Journal of Early Childhood, 37(1), 27–38.

OECD (2004) *Starting strong curricular and pedagogies in Early Childhood Education and Care: Five curriculum outlines.* Paris: OECD. Available at **www.oecd.org/dataoecd/23/36/31672150.pdf** (accessed 1 May 2009).

Office of the United Nations High Commissioner for Human Rights (2007) *Report on Activities and Results.* Available at **www.ohchr.org/Documents/Press/OHCHR_Report_07_Full.pdf** (accessed 1 May 2009).

Paige-Smith, A (2004) Parent partnership and inclusion in the Early Years, in Miller, L and Devereux, J (eds) *Supporting children's learning in the Early Years.* London: David Fulton.

Penn, H (ed.) (2000) *Early childhood services: Theory, policy and practice.* Buckingham: Open University Press.

Pramling-Samuelson, I, Sheridan, S and Williams, P (2006) Five preschool curricula: Comparative perspectives. *International Journal of Early Education* 38, 1: 11–29.

Rinaldi, C (2006) *In dialogue with Reggio Emilia.* Abingdon: Routledge.

Siraj-Blatchford, I (2004) Quality teaching in the Early Years, in Anning, A, Cullen, J and Fleer, M (eds) (2004) *Early childhood education: Society and culture.* London: Sage Publications.

Sylva, K, Melhuish, E, Sammons, P, Siraj-Blatchford, I and Taggart, B (2004) *The Effective Provision of Pre-School Education Project.* Nottingham: DfES Publications.

UNESCO (2005) *Towards knowledge societies.* Available at **unesdoc.unesco.org** (accessed 1 May 2009).

UNICEF (2008) *Unite for children: Early childhood.* Available at **www.unicef.org/early childhood/index_3870.html** (accessed 1 May 2009).

Chapter 3

Primary practices and curriculum comparisons

Jackie Barbera and Deirdre Hewitt

Learning outcomes

By the end of this chapter you should be able to:

- understand the policy and practice of primary education and schooling and the issues surrounding this in England;
- be aware of how this policy and practice compares and contrasts to other countries, with particular reference to Romania and the Republic of Ireland;
- recognise how government initiatives influence and direct primary schools;
- be able to debate the nature and purpose of primary education while voicing your own informed views.

Chapter outline

English society generally accepts that children will go to school for their formal education and training to prepare them for their future life. In England this begins with primary education (sometimes referred to internationally as elementary education) when children are about four years of age. This education system builds on children's early years experiences in their home, with child minders, in nurseries or playgroups and ensures children are given a foundation in many necessary life skills such as basic literacy, numeracy and social skills which subsequently will be developed as children get older and gain formal qualifications in later sectors of education. The importance of primary education for the well-being of all children and as a foundation for their development to adulthood cannot be overestimated. Even within the United Kingdom there are significant differences in the provision of primary education from that in England, which is possibly the most regulated system in the world. This chapter gives you a brief overview of the historical development of the English primary system, its structure, curriculum and assessment practices. Romania provides an interesting contrast to England as it is a rapidly changing country. One needs to have some understanding of the political background to Romania, as it illuminates the present situation. Nicolae Ceauşescu's communist rule came to an end towards the end of 1989; this had a major impact on all areas of life, including education. The subsequent drive to join the European Union has had an effect upon education development. Despite Ireland's geographical location making it virtually England's neighbour, it has significant differences in education, making an interesting contrast. The difference begins with the compulsory school age as children in Ireland start school at the age of six and schooling is compulsory until the age of 16. Comparisons with these two countries are made which offer interesting reflections on the primary education in England and in the wider international context.

Primary schooling in England

Today primary education is widely accepted by society as the norm in England. However, if we look at the historical context, the system we have in place today has actually evolved over a relatively short period of time.

The history of modern Education has been dominated by the period from 1870 since this was a symbolic 'moment' of huge transition leading to the present order of things.

Bartlett and Barton, 2007, page 59

The development of this English educational system over the last 200 years, and particularly the focus for primary education, can be summed up by Table 3.1.

Table 3.1

Period	Focus of primary education policy development
1800–1870	towards state education for all children
1870–1902	the first stages of elementary schooling and schooling became compulsory for young children from five years of age
1902–1944	establishing education authorities and secondary schools
1944–1965	universal secondary education – the tripartite system and the 11-plus
1965–1988	comprehensive schooling and abolishment of the 11-plus
1988–2000	diversity and competition – establishing structural and curriculum changes including key stages, the National Curriculum, Literacy and Numeracy strategies and inspection and league tables
2000 to present day	establishing the early years foundation stage and curriculum, inclusion and personalised learning agenda through Every Child Matters, Primary National Strategies

It was not until the Public Education Bill of 1820 that education for the masses was promoted. Up until this time schooling was still very much voluntary and largely run by the church or private individuals and guilds. As Bartlett and Barton (2007) point out, these early schools of the 1800s were for working-class children and were a means of providing strict training in literacy and numeracy for large numbers of pupils as quickly as possible. As this elementary schooling began to gather momentum across the country there was a greater need for funding for the provision and in schools managers were encouraged to claim grants for children attending.

In 1870 the government realised that it needed to be more forceful in encouraging a national system of education and passed the Elementary Education Act, known as the Forster Act. This allowed for towns and cities to provide schools for five- to twelve-year-olds, funded by local government, with additional funding from central government dependent on inspection results. It ensured that in areas where there was little or inadequate provision that partially funded state board schools were established. The use of public funds demanded a level of accountability of teachers and schools. The school boards who ran these schools needed to ensure that their teacher employees could provide a far better quality of education than previously, whereby pupils would be able to read and write with fluency and expression and have knowledge of basic mathematics, up to and including fractions. By 1880 all children between the ages of five and ten years old were required to attend school (Bartlett and Barton, 2007). The Haddow Report of 1926 subsequently recommended the transition from primary schools to secondary schools at age 11. This gave rise to the national system of state education we have today, where pupils begin primary school ahead of their fifth birthday and transfer to secondary education at 11. Successive education acts made education compulsory. The Butler Act of 1944 raised the school leaving age to 15 and by 1972 this was raised to 16. The government plans to raise the minimum school leaving age to 18 in England from 2013. Interestingly, however, it is likely to remain at 16 in Scotland and Wales.

Primary education in England

The 1988 Education Reform Act gave rise to many of the systems, procedures and policies that are used to run primary schools in England today. This act arose out of a period of much criticism of standards in schools and was seen by government as a means of raising standards of pupil achievement and making schools more accountable. Policies developing from this included the introduction of a national curriculum, a more rigid approach to the curriculum. There was much tighter government control of schools in England, where the curriculum became a legal requirement for all pupils aged between 5 and 16. The literacy and numeracy strategies developed from this a few years later. The introduction of a national curriculum was intended to establish an entitlement for all pupils to a coherent and continuous curriculum irrespective of place of schooling, background, race, culture, gender, ability or disability (Clark and Waller, 2007) and to ensure pupils' progess was measured against the same set descriptors and attainment targets. An intense focus on assessment of pupils began and, alongside teacher assessment, the SATs (Statutory Assessment Tests) were 'born' to measure individual schools' performance in delivering the core national curriculum subjects (mathematics, literacy and science). League tables were published, giving performance figures for all schools, thus naming and so shaming schools with poor pupil performance. Many also saw this as an assessment of school effectiveness and teacher performance and a move towards performance-related pay (Hayes, 2004). To return more responsibility to schools and local authorities, and in a bid to ensure accountability, a major development from the 1988 Act was the joint administration of schools by local authorities and central government. This central government body, the Department for Children, Schools and Families (DCSF), works with local authorities, many of whom have relinquished some of their power to schools. As such, schools are now able to have far more control over their management, particularly in financial matters. At a national level, the DCSF is responsible for ensuring the implementation by schools and local authorities of all education policies and legislation made by the government; it does this through its inspection of schools which is carried out by the Office for Standards in Education (OFSTED) and teams of trained Inspectors.

At the start of the new millennium there were further changes to primary schools as 'extended services' were introduced beyond the traditional school day, as the welfare of children and inclusion became a social focus. Much of this arose from a recognition that for some children education was much more than just learning subjects and that life skills and life-long learning needed to be high on the agenda for education inthe uncertain economic climate of the early twenty-first century. The publication of *Every Child Matters* in 2003 and the subsequent Children's Act of 2004 has brought to the forefront the need for primary schools to personalise learning and really view education as the development of the whole child and not just as the teaching of traditional academic subjects.

Reflective Task

The nature of primary education in England

Read the following case study carefully:

It's seven-thirty in the morning and some parents are already arriving with their children at Bowform Street School. As the door is opened they are greeted with the smell of toast and the sounds of children playing. For many the day begins with breakfast club, ensuring that the children are getting a healthy start to their day and parents can go to work in the knowledge that their children are safe and happy. The headteacher and staff arrive. Classrooms are prepared ready for the busy school day. A parent brings in a distressed child and a teacher meets with the parent and child in order to support both parent and child.

As the children arrive at the nursery with their parent or carer they are greeted by the teacher and support workers. Typically, the children hang up their coats on their personalised name peg before entering a vibrant, colourful classroom area displaying their own creative work. There are a variety of activities set up for the day, which include sand and water play, paint, jigsaws, seed planting and dressing up. The children eagerly choose an activity designed to stimulate them. When all the children have arrived, they are gathered together to plan their day.

In Year 6, where the children are 10 and 11 years old, they arrive at school with their friends, chatting about the previous evening. When they reach class they hang up their coats, put personal possessions in their tray and sign in for packed lunch or school dinner. The classroom has tables for six children to group around and discuss work. There is a quiet reading area with scatter cushions, a shared art area and a number of computers which are available for use throughout the day. Wall displays reflect the children's current topic work. They are sitting in friendship groups around tables of four to six competing to solve the early morning challenge set by the teacher.

At 9.15, the children and staff gather together as a group in the hall to formally begin their day, with a celebration of life through song, drama and readings. This community ethos, which is promoted by the headteacher, sets the scene for the day, a scene which expects children and staff to be caring and supportive of each other whilst each striving for their own and each other's success. Formal classes then begin with literacy and mathematics occupying the morning session.

How does this account of the start to a typical day compare with primary schools you have experienced? Summarise the differences and similarities.

The primary curriculum and assessment in England

The National Curriculum imposed a common course of study and linked assessment for pupils in all primary and secondary schools. So profound was this change that over the next few years teachers grappled with the introduction of a new range of key vocabulary and national strategies and initiatives. These changes saw the introduction of Key Stages:

- Foundation Stage for three- to five-year-olds (non-compulsory until the child is 5).
- Key Stage 1 for five- to seven-year-olds.
- Key Stage 2 for seven- to eleven-year-olds.

Core and foundation subjects were also identified in the National Curriculum, to be taught across all key stages, and assessed through the SATs:

- Core:
  English
  Maths
  Science
  Information and Communication Technology (ICT)
- Foundation:
  Art
  Design and Technology
  Geography
  History
  Music
  PE
  RE (a statutory subject with non–statutory content).

All of this resulted in children being categorised in terms of attainment levels in the SATs and their progress linked to individual specific target setting. This change was a move by the government to increase the standardisation and uniformity of schooling, especially in terms of the curriculum and the teaching methods used.

The development of this curriculum and teachers' perceptions about how it should be delivered have been influenced over the years by many educationalists and theorists. The most significant of these for primary education are Skinner, Bruner, Vygotsky and Piaget. The development of these social constructivism theories are really the foundation of much of the curriculum work that has happened in schools over the last 50 years with the emphasis being on learning rather than teaching – a model that Moore (2000) identifies as having become labelled as *progressive, constructivist* and *child-centred*. Moore identifies that:

while reference to key educational theorists may be absent from much official documentation, there is no doubt that their work has . . . often lent credence and implicit support to official policy to government commissioned reports, surveys, and to teachers' own philosophies and practice.

Moore, 2000, page 3

Indeed Moore gives a very good overview of how these theorists have influenced teaching and learning and how these link to curriculum development and delivery.

Although schools are required to deliver the National Curriculum and are inspected as to their ability to do this there is no doubt that significant learning also takes place through what might be called the 'hidden' curriculum. This is what children learn outside the formal curriculum, for example, through the people they encounter, the way in which the school is run and their work is organised, or the materials they are given. This all contributes to the ethos of the school and through this children are encouraged to have specific attitudes and values. This is largely led by the management style of the school and the staff involved. Life messages are often conveyed accidentally and incidentally and it is important that all those working with children appreciate the significance of this:

The curriculum is everything that is actively sponsored, or else condoned, by the school and its teachers, whether it is on the timetable or not.

Wragg, 1997, page 23

Reflective Task

The National Curriculum

The learning that the nation has decided to set before its young in England is called the National Curriculum and full details can be found on the Qualifications and Curriculum Authority (QCA) website. Visit **www.qca.org.uk**, follow links to the curriculum *and, focusing on Key Stages 1 and 2, answer the following:*

- *How can you be assured that the information on this website is reliable?*
- Which National Curriculum subjects are statutory (compulsory) and which are non-statutory?
- What is meant by *General Teaching Requirements?*
- What might be the implications of these requirements for teachers?
- *For a statutory* National Curriculum subject of your choice how are teachers advised to assess individual children? (Keep this in mind as you read on in this chapter).
- In your own words, summarise the values and purposes underpinning the National Curriculum in England. To what extent were you aware of such values in your own schooling?

Since the introduction of the National Curriculum (1988) there have been numerous reviews and critiques of it. One of the most recent and most significant was led by Alexander and Cambridge University, *The Cambridge Primary Review*. This was an independent review of the primary curriculum.

The report found a number of key positive elements:

- *There is widespread acceptance of the need for a national curriculum, and the promise of entitlement which it embodies.*
- *There have been significant gains from the national curriculum since its introduction in 1989, notably in science, citizenship and the handling of values and children's personal development.*
- *The national primary, literacy and numeracy strategies (especially the latter) have many supporters, and younger teachers in particular welcome the structure and guidance which they provide.*
- *The Early Years Foundation Stage (EYFS) areas of learning and development provide an appropriate platform for primary education.*

University of Cambridge Faculty of Education, 2009a, b

However, it also found many negative elements, such as pressure at specific points of primary schooling with the narrowing of the curriculum to enable standards for testing to be met. It also suggested that too great a focus on literacy and mathematics has decontextualised these subjects and they need to now be taught in a much more cross-curricular context, particularly in the case of English. The review also noted that curriculum debate has been lacking amongst teachers and this has led to weakened curriculum practice. They called for the curriculum to differentiate *national* and *community* needs, allowing for greater regional and local flexibility and creativity.

A second recent and significant review, the *Independent Review of the Primary Curriculum*, was led by Sir Jim Rose and commissioned by the Department for Children, Schools and Families. Rose's interim report (December 2008), suggests what is needed for the Primary curriculum is:

a curriculum design based on a clear set of culturally derived aims and values, which promote challenging subject teaching alongside equally challenging cross-curricular studies. Placing literacy, numeracy, ICT and personal development at its heart, the provisional model aims to secure high achievement in these vital skills for learning and life. Six areas of learning are proposed to give schools optimum flexibility to localise the curriculum and respond to children's different but developing abilities, to provide ample opportunities for cross-curricular and discrete teaching and to help smooth the transition from the Early Years Foundation Stage to the primary curriculum.

Rose, 2008

It will be interesting to see how these reviews impact on primary curriculum development and policy making over the oncoming years. One can be sure, however, that primary education in England will continue to change and evolve as teachers and politicians reflect on practice and strive to support the development of a workforce for tomorrow.

Primary education in Romania

The Romanian education system, although compulsory, is far less formal and less government-regulated than that in England. The education system in Romania has undergone many transformations, particularly following the end of the communist era. The removal of political education from the curriculum in 1990 marked the beginning of the development of new approaches to education which, to a large extent, reflect the importance placed by many Romanians on being well educated. In1995, the Ministry of Education and Research assumed responsibility for the education system. There followed a period of considerable change with new legislation being brought in most years, often reversing decisions made only a few years previously, as the government sought to quickly modernise the country through education. Romania is still a country in transition, and this in itself brings problems. One of these is the levels of poverty in certain areas, usually rural districts, which can result in low levels of pupil enrolment. This situation is not specific to Romania, as current studies indicate that poverty has a direct correlation with education internationally: *poverty is a major indicator of likely low participation and performance for both gender* (Collins, Kenway and McLeod, 2000, page 76).

The effects of poverty are experienced in England, but in Romania the scale of poverty is significantly greater and so its effects are more widely felt. Figures reveal that:

Even by 2002 three out of every ten Romanians were poor; one out of ten, extremely poor. At the same time, there is a strong positive association between economic growth and poverty reduction. Several variables predict poverty, but multivariate regressions show that the key correlate of poverty is education, with Roma ethnicity and being unemployed second and third in importance, respectively. Rural residents have more than double the probability of being poor than urban residents and rural areas account for 67 percent of total poverty.

Berryman *et al.*, 2007

Schooling in Romania is now provided free of charge by the state but in many cases the family still has to buy books and pencils and so on, often serving to prohibit access for some families who cannot afford to pay for such items. In order to address this issue there is a government initiative Rural Education Project which aims to reduce inequities between rural and urban schools that were contributing to high levels of poverty in rural areas.

Romania was one of the first European countries to undergo large-scale educational reform: one of its goals being to introduce a flexible national curriculum. Post-1998 and the communist regime, it was realised that the education system did not suit the political or social democracy which had now entered the Romanian domain. In other words, politics can be seen as a driver of education. This is comparable to England, when one party brings in educational reform which might then be overturned by the next political party in power. This explains why education is context-bound. During communism the educational climate was very teacher-centred; facts had to be taught and memorised by children, and knowledge was ideological. Children were not allowed to question and teachers were not allowed to exercise any creativity. With the overthrow of communism and the event of democracy, a different education system was required. Children were encouraged to question, and to be able to problem solve. Memorisation of facts was no longer enough. As a result, basic pedagogy had to change. This example helps us to appreciate why education has to change, why new policies have to be introduced: to reflect the changing nature of society. All subject matter for the new curriculum was aimed at developing higher-order thinking skills. The reformed curriculum reflects modern culture, with attention being paid to developing competencies, skills and attitudes. Teachers were, for the first time since 1989, allowed to use their own creativity, and to have some choice of textbooks. This reference to textbooks once more reflects a change in political direction, due to the fact that under communism only certain textbooks were allowed to be used by the school and these were extremely limited. There was one textbook per subject per grade; furthermore, there was no choice. In addition, the books were of a very poor quality. Just think of the number of books available to teachers in England, with more being published every year. This is only now beginning to be the case in many parts of Romania.

Primary curriculum and assessment in Romania

Internationally, there is considerable variation in the emphasis given at the primary stage to a variety of subjects such as science, information technology, foreign languages, the humanities and the arts. These variations are largely informed by cultural differences in educational values, with countries like England pursuing an increasingly instrumental and skills-based primary curriculum while others show a greater interest in the child's all-round development and understanding. The Romanian primary curriculum is strongly academic and can also be very rigid. It comprises 15 compulsory subjects and up to five optional subjects. However, unlike in England, these optional subjects are chosen by the school rather than by the government. In addition a National Assessment and Examination system has been established.

Under the reform, it was decided that assessments and examinations should meet three purposes: certification, selection, and providing feedback on the learning performance of the system for the public. These objectives have been met and exceeded.

Berryman *et al.*, 2007

The following table summarises subjects each child must take:

Table 3.2 Romanian primary school curriculum

Subject	Required years of primary study
Romanian, Mathematics, Art, PE	8
Religion	up to 8
First foreign language (usually English, French or German)	7 or 8
Geography, History	6
Second foreign language (English, French, German, Spanish, Italian, Russian or Portuguese)	3 or 4
Civic Education, Physics, Biology	3
Chemistry	2
IT (although in many schools this can be studied throughout the 8 years)	2

Traditionally families, particularly in more suburban areas, have been very involved in their children's education, supporting them to achieve good results. However, some variables have considerable effect on education and access to provision, and are often linked to economic income. These variables include being a member of a minority ethnic community, poverty, disability, size of family and whether or not the parents have had a good education (Berryman *et al.*, 2007). There is also significant evidence of segregation, for instance some ethnic groups, such as Roma children, are often taught in separate classes from the mainstream, due to the significant prejudices that can exist within Romanian communities.

A child's experience of education in a city school is very different from that in a rural school. City schools are usually well equipped and have good facilities. This contrasts greatly with some rural schools where sometimes, in very small villages, children are only offered four years of schooling, then have to travel to the nearest large village for the remainder of their education. This is a barrier to continuing education for many children, not least because parents are often unable to afford the necessary transport.

Practical Task

An example of rural education in Romania

Read the personal account below of an observation of a school setting in a rural location in Romania.

Students sat at crudely-fashioned wooden desks, few materials adorned the walls, the school was ill-maintained, and the teacher's cupboard was nearly bare of learning materials. Though we entered the school in the middle of a session there were no materials on their desks (the teacher informed me they could not afford these items). There were no toilet facilities, nor running water, and the students were released for the day shortly after we arrived (at about 12:30 pm). Grades one and three were in one room while two and four were in the other; one of the teachers explained that the classes were structured this way in order to divide the burden of teaching young students to read between the two teachers.

Berryman *et al.*, 2007, page 80.

Consider how this compares and contrasts to the similarities and differences you identified above in the case study of an English school.

Primary education in Ireland

The current legislation governing school attendance in the Republic of Ireland is the Education Welfare Act of 2000 (DES 2000). This act made education compulsory for all children from the ages of six to sixteen or until three years of post-primary education has been completed, whichever is the later. The primary education sector in Ireland comprises different types of primary school:

- denominational (faith) schools;
- multi-denominational (mixed-faith) schools;
- Irish-speaking schools (called *Gaelscoileanna*);
- special schools;
- non-State-aided private primary schools.

Education in state primary schools in Ireland is free of charge, as it is in England and Romania. Schools are funded by the Government and supplemented by local contributions. The primary school cycle is eight years long, two years of infant classes (junior and senior), followed by class 1 to class 6. Parents are required to ensure that their children attend a recognised school or receive a certain minimum education from the age of six to the age of sixteen. As in England, there is no legal obligation on children to attend school nor on their parents to send them to school but there is a legal obligation to ensure a child receives an education. The Irish Constitution allows education to be provided in the home and does not explicitly require the state to define minimum standards.

Primary curriculum and assessment in Ireland

In Ireland the current Primary School Curriculum was introduced in 1999. It is taught in all schools and is regulated by the National Council for Curriculum and Assessment (NCCA). Primary education in Ireland places great emphasis on the individual child and encourages a curriculum that is relevant to the needs and interests of the child. It also promotes an integrated curriculum with pedagogy being centred around guided learning and discovery. The curriculum emphasises the importance of literacy, numeracy, and language, while at the same time responding to changing needs in science and technology, social personal and health education, and citizenship.

The curriculum covers 11 subjects divided into six subject areas:

Table 3.3 Republic of Ireland primary school curriculum

Subject Area	Specific Subjects
Language	English, Gaelic
Mathematics	Mathematics
Social Environmental and Scientific Education (SESE)	History, Geography, Science
Arts Education	Visual Arts, Drama, Music
Physical Education	PE
Social, Personal and Health Education (SPHE)	Social, Personal and Health Education

All 11 subjects are taught throughout the 8 years of primary education. Religious Education is also included in the primary curriculum but remains the responsibility of the different church authorities.

> ### Critical Thinking Task 🕴
>
> **The Irish primary curriculum**
>
> The National Council for Curriculum and Assessment (NCCA) is committed to improving the quality of education in Ireland through continuous review of curriculum and assessment provision. Visit the NCCA's website, **www.ncca.ie**, *and, focusing on Primary Education, consider the following:*
>
> - *Compare and contrast the* aims of primary education in the Republic of Ireland with such aims in England and Romania.
> - *What are the defining features of Irish primary education?*
> - *Critically compare these defining features to the key features of the English and Romanian systems. What are the implications for teachers in these countries?*

Although the curriculum in the Republic of Ireland is similar in content to England, it differs in its approach to assessment. It focuses mainly on Assessment for Learning (AFL) and Assessment of Learning (AOL). The teacher periodically records a child's progress in order to identify his/her learning and development and to compile a report for parents. This is a much less rigid form of assessment than standardised tests; however, there is some statutory, standardised testing in Ireland:

All Irish primary schools are required to administer standardised tests in English and mathematics to their pupils twice during their primary school years – at the end of first class or beginning of second class and at the end of fourth class or beginning of fifth class. The tests are usually administered by the class teacher under conditions specified in the test's manual, in order to ensure that the test results are valid. Teachers mark and score the tests as set out in the test manual.

NCCA, 2009

As set out in *Supporting Assessment in Primary School* (Department of Education and Science Circular letter, 0138/2006), from 2007 all Irish primary schools are required to administer standardised tests in English and mathematics to their pupils twice during their primary school years:

- At the end of first class OR at the beginning of second class AND
- At the end of fourth class OR at the beginning of fifth class.

Sociological *Perspective*

Primary schooling

Your thinking so far has been directed towards the intellectual development of the child. However, national and international educational systems claim to be child-centred and holistic, and therefore primary schools are also concerned with the social and emotional development of children. With this in mind consider the following reflective task.

Reflective Task

School ethos

The ethos of a school is a reflection of the way pupils relate to each other, how pupils relate to staff, and how the school relates to the community it serves. For most schools this will be determined by the headteacher and governing body. Nowadays many schools express this through an explicit mission statement.

An internet search quickly shows that primary school mission statements vary, some are short and succinct and others considerably longer. Some examples of the former include:

- *Opening minds, unlocking potential, celebrating success together.*
- *An inclusive community of life-long learners.*
- *Working in partnership with parents to promote the spiritual, moral, cultural, mental and physical development of all pupils.*
- *Maximising potential in a safe and friendly environment.*
- *Helping children to live as good Christians, supporting and enabling them to reach their full potential and empowering them to be caring individuals capable of critical independent thought.*
- *We are committed to ongoing development in striving for excellence and in delivering the highest quality education within a caring school.*

Look at the mission statements above. In pairs, consider responses to these:

- What indication do these mission statements give you about what the school might be like?
- Try writing a mission statement either for a primary school you know or your ideal school.
- What might a mission statement for a primary school in Romania or the Republic of Ireland be?

When should children start primary school?

The age at which children should start their formal schooling is much debated and contested across the world. Many educationalists have particularly strong views on this especially those with an interest in early years education.

Statutory ages of primary schooling in England

Primary Education in England currently covers three stages:

- Foundation Stage (ages three to five);
- Key Stage 1 (ages five to seven);
- Key Stage 2 (ages seven to eleven).

Key Stage 1 starts the September before a child's fifth birthday but attendance is only compulsory once the child is five.

Statutory ages of primary schooling in Romania

Primary education in Romania currently covers two stages:

• kindergarten (optional for ages three to six); compulsory schooling (ages six to ten or eleven).

In Romania the statutory school starting age is six years old. This was reduced from seven in 2003 when the period of compulsory education in Romania was extended from eight to ten years. Children younger than six have the option to attend a kindergarten for nursery education. Nursery begins at the age of three, and ends at six or seven, depending on the child's achievement. At the end of nursery, children are assessed by the school that they will attend; primary education starts at the age of six or seven, depending on the individual child's level of development, and ends at ten or eleven. One of the issues for Romanian education is that there are limited places for public kindergartens, with long waiting lists. Numbers of private kindergarten places are increasing rapidly but the cost prohibits access for many families.

Statutory ages of primary schooling in Ireland

Primary Education in Ireland currently covers three stages:

• Junior infants (ages four to five);
• Senior infants (ages five to six);
• Primary 1 to Primary 6 (ages six to twelve).

In Ireland, like Romania, children are not obliged to attend school until the age of six. However, over half of four-year-olds and most five-year-olds are enrolled in the infant classes in primary school. As a result, much of what is regarded as early childhood education in other countries is included in Ireland's primary school system.

Practical Task

School starting ages in Europe

Different countries have differing views on when formal education should become compulsory. The low school admission age in England, particularly in comparison to other European countries, has been the centre of much debate. The main argument put forward in favour of the early starting age dates back to the late nineteenth century when the need to protect young children from their family's expectations that they would go out to work was a major concern, as were the unhealthy conditions encountered by children on the streets. At the same time, employers were appeased by establishing an early school *leaving* age so that children could enter the workforce (Woodhead, 1989).

Subsequent legislation confirmed that parents must ensure their children attend full-time education from the start of the term following their fifth birthday. In recent years schools have increasingly been admitting children at the beginning of the year in which they became five. This was made possible by the falling birth rate but the benefits of this policy have been supported by research looking at the achievements of children born at different times of the year. It would appear that some of the children in the year group do statistically less well in some aspects of school than peers that are born earlier in the year (Sharp, 2002). This 'summer-born' effect meant that, until recently, such children often had a much shorter first year at primary school. This is now used by local authorities as an influential argument in favour of annual admission policies.

Have a look at the summary table for Europe below (Table 3.4).

Table 3.4 School compulsory starting ages in Europe (2007)

Age	Country
Four	Northern Ireland
Five	England, Holland, Malta, Scotland, Wales
Six	Austria, Belgium, Cyprus, Czech Republic, France, Germany, Greece, Hungary, Iceland, Republic of Ireland, Italy, Liechtenstein, Luxembourg, Norway, Portugal, Romania, Slovakia, Slovenia, Spain, Turkey
Seven	Bulgaria, Denmark, Estonia, Finland, Latvia, Lithuania, Poland, Sweden

Working as a group:

- Each member of the group should select a different country with a school-starting age other than five.
- Search the internet and/or other sources of information to find out what rationale your chosen country puts forward for this decision.
- In your group compare the different starting ages and the rationale for their selection.
- What is the evidence presented by the different countries to support the starting age?
- What implications, if any, does this evidence have for the starting age in England?

What age a child should start primary school depends, to a large extent, on the nature of the schooling, what it is the child will actually experience on a daily basis.

Chapter Summary

This chapter has presented a number of key themes in primary education at the start of the twenty-first century, namely, the school starting age, the place of a national curriculum and formal testing of pupils. It has presented the position of each theme in primary schools in England, Romania and Ireland. It raises questions about the nature and purpose of primary education. Is it to develop children intellectually, or is there a place for social and emotional development? Should the holistic nature of the child be attended to?

- There is strong government commitment to the development of this key phase of education in the vast majority of countries and certainly in the three discussed above.
- The primary curriculum varies from country to country and is strongly influenced, sometimes controlled, by national governments.
- The content of the curriculum and favoured teaching styles are influenced by the country's view on the nature and purpose of primary education.
- Pupil assessment is tightly linked to the curriculum. Some countries have very rigid national assessment regimes while others allow for greater teacher assessment.

Research focus

Task 1

Alexander in his recent, seminal book compares primary education in five countries. It is an excellent piece of comparative education and is highly recommended to you:

- Alexander, R (2001) *Culture and pedagogy: International comparisons in primary education*. Oxford: Blackwell Publishing.

The book begins with a fascinating description: a snapshot of primary schooling in the five countries involved, America, England, France, India and Russia. Read this section, pages 9 to 14. Make careful notes to further your knowledge or understanding of the key themes discussed in this chapter.

Task 2

If you are interested in researching the curriculum further and comparative views of it then you should read Chapter 9, 'The Idea of a School' in Alexander's book above. It discusses how, for example, the routines of the day, the gender balance of the staff, and the way pupils are grouped all combine together to create the hidden curriculum referred to in this chapter. These key organisational factors all help to create and reinforce the ethos of the school and are, to a large extent, outside the control of the government and any formal national curriculum. Read this chapter and make notes relating Alexander's examples to any of your own experiences.

References

Alexander, R (2001) *Culture and pedagogy: International comparisons in primary education*. London: Blackwell.

Bartlett, S and Barton, D (2007) *Introduction to education studies*. London: Sage.

Berryman, S, Gove, A, Sapatoru, D and Tirca, A (2007) *A country case study: Evaluation of the World Bank's assistance to basic education in Romania*. Washington: World Bank.

Clark, M and Waller, T (eds) (2007) *Early childhood education and care policy and practice*. London: Sage.

Collins, C, Kenway, J and McLeod, J (2000) *Factors influencing the educational performance of males and females in school and their initial destinations after leaving school*. Deakin: University of South Australia. Available at: **www.dest.gov.au/NR/rdonlyres/F0270F6EB 2C3–4CF4–833D-4C8029EA7D6E/4093/Gender_Report.pdf** (accessed 20 January 2009)

Department of Education and Science [DES] (2000) Education (Welfare) Act. Available at: **www.education.ie/servlet/blobservlet/act_22_2000.pdf** (accessed 6 May 2009).

Hayes, D (2004) *Foundations of primary teaching*, 3rd ed. London: David Fulton.

Moore, A (2000) *Teaching and learning: Pedagogy, curriculum and culture, key issues in teaching and learning*. London: RoutledgeFalmer.

NCCA (2009) *Primary Curriculum Review Phase 2*. Available at: **www.ncca.ie** (accessed 6 May 2009).

Rose J (2008) *Interim report of the Independent Review of the Primary Curriculum*. Available at: **www.dcsf.gov.uk/primarycurriculumreview** (accessed 6 May 2009).

Sharp, C (2002) *Schools starting age: European policy and recent research*. Paper presented at Local Government Association Seminar, 'When Should Our Children Start School?', London, 1 November. Available at: **www.nfer.ac.uk/publications/other-publications/ conference-papers/pdf_docs/PaperSSF.pdf** (accessed 6 May 2009).

University of Cambridge Faculty of Education (2009) *Towards a new primary curriculum: A report from the Cambridge Primary Review. Part 1: Past and present.* Cambridge: University of Cambridge Faculty of Education. Available at: **www.primaryreview.org.uk/Downloads/ CPR_Curric_rep_Pt1_Past_Present.pdf** (accessed 6 May 2009).

University of Cambridge Faculty of Education (2009) *Towards a new primary curriculum: A report from the Cambridge Primary Review. Part 2: the future.* Cambridge: University of Cambridge Faculty of Education. Available at: **www.primaryreview.org.uk/Downloads/ CPR_Curric_rep_Pt2_Future.pdf** (accessed 6 May 2009).

Woodhead, M (1989) The rationale for changing admission policies in England and Wales. *Journal of Education Policy* 4, 1: 1–21.

Wragg, AC (1997) *The cubic curriculum*. London: Routledge.

Chapter 4

High schools and high stakes assessments

Anthony Edwards

Learning outcomes

By the end of this chapter you should be able to:

- identify some contemporary educational issues and trends in secondary education;
- understand something of what influences the development of secondary education;
- develop an understanding of secondary education in England and Finland;
- use appropriate statistical sources of information – including TIMSS (Trends in International Mathematics and Science Study), PISA (Programme for International Student Assessment) and PIRLS (*Progress in International Reading Literacy Study*) – to compare the performance of different education systems.

Chapter outline

This chapter explores secondary education, defined here as that offered to pupils aged 11 to 16. In particular it compares the English and Finnish systems, looking at data gathered by international assessment programmes. In order to do this effectively both the current English and Finnish systems of secondary education will be examined in depth. England rather than the United Kingdom is explored here because the Trends in International Mathematics and Science Study (TIMSS) and Programme for International Student Assessment (PISA) surveys report on the constituent countries of the UK rather than the whole. It also represents a country that is struggling with the key challenges that face educators today.

Finland has been selected, despite its relatively small size and decision not to take part in TIMSS, because it scores highest in PISA surveys and is often heralded as a beacon of outstanding educational practice. A third international assessment survey, *Progress in International Reading Literacy Study (PIRLS)*, will also be examined although its focus is on ten-year-olds, so it considers primary, rather than secondary achievement. The question of whether or not meaningful international comparisons of this type can be undertaken at all will be explored throughout.

International comparisons of what secondary pupils from different countries achieve in literacy, mathematics and science are regularly undertaken by a number of agencies including the International Association for the Evaluation of Educational Achievement (IAE), the European Commission (EU) and the Organisation for Economic Cooperation and Development (OECD). These types of investigation may vary in terms of their scale and the nature of the evidence gathered but they are increasingly used to either justify the educational policies and practices in different systems or condemn them. As a result of globalisation policymakers and educators are increasingly tempted to use:

international comparisons to assess how well national systems of education are perform-ing. These comparisons shed light on a host of policy issues, from access to education and equity of resources to the quality of school outputs.

IES National Centre for Education Statistics, 2008

They can make governments quiver, journalists run to file copy and educators very angry, influencing how funds are allocated and laws related to education are shaped. They can have a bearing on how teachers are perceived by the wider community because the results are sometimes transposed beyond the world of those with a professional interest in education into headlines in the press. This chapter examines the workings of such surveys and the results they generate from an English and Finnish perspective, in particular. Specifically it will:

- explore what TIMSS, PISA and PIRLS are;
- identify how they gather their evidence;
- examine what the implications of the results they generate might be.

Critical Thinking Task

Can pupil assessments be compared across countries?

The International Association for the Evaluation of Educational Achievement (IAE) believes that international comparison is ubiquitous in modern life. It notes that we are surrounded by league tables on everything from national wealth to obesity rates and that education is no exception. The Secretary General of the OECD (2007) asserts that by monitoring education internationally within an agreed framework, valid comparisons can take place and ambitious goals set for educators. Yet this form of monitoring is not universally welcomed. Some believe that because education is about developing the individual, league tables are invidious. Others point out that it is very difficult to produce meaningful comparative information in education, particularly between countries which are at different stages of development. When measuring the literacy levels, is it fair to directly compare the performance of those nations which have speakers of many different first languages with those in which there is one mother tongue? How do you account for the effect of perceived national attitudes towards mathematics and science on individual performance in those subjects? The IAE argues that the sceptics are wrong. They emphatically state that valid and useful comparative information on pupil achievement across different countries can be assembled simply by doing it, despite the challenges (Hegarty, 2004).

Reflecting on what you know about comparative education, do you think it possible to meaningfully compare one education system with another? Consider by listing:

- the benefits that might accrue from undertaking an activity of this type successfully, such as helping to shape future education policy; the challenges you might encounter, such as language barriers; what points of comparison you might apply, for example within subjects like mathematics;
- which countries would be best to compare with your own, for example do you choose those with similar populations?

Trends in International Mathematics and Science Study (TIMSS)

Since its inception in 1959, the IEA has conducted more than 23 international studies into achievement of school-aged children in mathematics, science, language, civics, and reading. The TIMSS project emerged from this long series of studies, involves testing pupils between 9 to 10 and 13 to 14 years of age (and occasionally at the end of secondary education) from different countries in mathematics and science. The first TIMSS survey (which at the time stood for Third International Mathematics and Science Study) in 1995 was the largest and most ambitious study of comparative education ever undertaken and involved 45 countries and nearly 500,000 students. Surveys of varying sizes have been conducted every four years since then. Plans to implement end-of-school advanced tests continue to emerge. The data collected is used to identify pupil achievement and reasons are also sought to explain any difference in results between countries that may occur. The project is funded by those participating, with support from the World Bank, the United States Department of Education through the National Center for Education Statistics, and the United Nations Development Programme. The project is co-ordinated by a consortium made up of the IEA International Study Center (USA), the IEA Secretariat (Holland), IEA Data Processing Centre (Germany), Statistics Canada and the Educational Testing Service (USA). National centres in participating countries complete the infrastructure. Any country which can afford it can take part. Schools are randomly selected by the consortium, who also specify which classes and students should take part.

The data gathered by the TIMSS project relates to the statutory or intended curriculum, the implemented (or what is actually taught) curriculum and the attained (or what pupils have learnt) curriculum. Students in every participating country are required to answer the same assessments and questionnaire translated into the language used for learning and teaching. Students complete a test book containing short-answer and extended questions on problem solving and an investigation in mathematics and science. They and their teachers also fill in mathematical and science-related questionnaires designed to provide a context for the resulting performance scores. The questionnaires elicit information on student attitudes to learning and social and work habits in and outside school. Teachers are also questioned on their attitudes and practices in learning and teaching and participation in professional development. School managers are asked to provide factual information about their educational organisations, such as size, and about policy, budget, pedagogical and curriculum issues as well. In addition data is collected periodically to provide performance benchmarks. An analysis of observations of Year 8 lessons in mathematics and science is sometimes undertaken. The assessments and questionnaires are designed to specifications in a guiding framework.

A panel of international experts in the teaching of mathematics and science and testing helps shape the form the assessment framework takes, in conjunction with representatives from national centres. Development of the tests begins with an analysis of the curriculum guides and textbooks from different countries to identify the priority topics. TIMSS results are reported on a scale from 0 to 1,000, with the majority of student scores falling between 200 and 800. Various statistical techniques are used to moderate these raw scores so that they better reflect what has actually been achieved. Comparison between mathematics and science scales is not possible.

Practical Task | 👥👥

Progress in International Reading Literacy

The following is an extract from a news report about the PIRLS survey. Read it and consider what it tells you about the particular survey and about England's performance.

England falls in reading league
The reading performance of children in England has fallen from third to nineteenth in the world in a major assessment. The Progress in International Reading Literacy Study (PIRLS), undertaken every five years, involved children aged about 10 in 40 countries. Scotland also fell, from fourteenth to twenty-sixth. Russia, which matched it last time, was top of the overall achievement table. Analysis of the England results said children were spending more time on computers and reading less for fun. PIRLS is designed to investigate children's 'reading literacy' and associated factors after, in most countries, four years of formal schooling – five in some including England and Scotland . . . After seeing the 2006 results the Children, Schools and Families Secretary said parents must do more.

Key findings:

- *Pupils in England achieved significantly above the international mean in PIRLS 2006 but significantly lower than some major European countries, including Italy and Germany.*
- *The performance of the three highest attaining countries in 2001 – Sweden, the Netherlands and England – was significantly lower in 2006.*
- *The three highest achieving countries in 2006 were the Russian Federation, Hong Kong and Singapore.*
- *In almost all countries, including England, girls achieved significantly higher mean scores than boys. In England, the performance of girls has fallen slightly more than that of boys, and the performance of both is significantly lower than in 2001.*

BBC, 2007

Divide into small groups, preferably in pairs. Now that you have read the report on England's results look at the PIRLS website for the results of other countries.

- Choose a country and look carefully at its results.
- Write a short newspaper report for your chosen country.

Programme for International Student Assessment (PISA)

The OECD undertakes a triennial survey of 15-year-olds in schools in all its member countries, and others co-opted for the purpose of the survey. PISA measures performance (literacy) in mathematics, reading and science. Work began on the infrastructure for PISA in the mid-1990s and it was officially launched in 1997. The first survey was carried out in 2000 with 43 countries. The main focus was on reading with a subsidiary focus on maths and science. In 2003, 41 countries participated, with the main focus that year on maths and the subsidiary focus on reading and science with the introduction of problem solving as a fourth element. In 2006, the number of countries participating increased to 56 with a main focus for that year on science and the subsidiary focus on maths and reading.

Each survey is managed by an international contractor appointed by the PISA governing board after a tendering process, and national project managers selected by participating countries.

Applications by countries who wish to be involved in a survey are vetted by the board. Those invited to take part must have the requisite infrastructure, be able to contribute to the cost of running the survey (PISA is funded exclusively by the participants) and join two years prior to a survey. A number of committees shape the details of each survey including:

- a subject-matter expert group (made up of world-renowned experts) which designs the theoretical framework;
- a questionnaire expert group which guides the construction of the questionnaires.

Typically between 4,500 and 5,000 randomly chosen students from each participating country take part. They undertake two-hour-long pencil and paper tests, a mixture of multiple-choice and open-ended questions, based on real-life situations. Further data on the economic and social backgrounds of pupils is gathered by questionnaires, as is information on the school. The OECD has developed a scale from 0 to 1,000 with five levels of proficiency to categorise the questions that are set and provide a framework for the results in each subject. Questions at Level 1, involving familiar contexts such as those associated with the immediate environment, routine procedures and simple actions require only the most basic skills to complete require students to answer. They get progressively harder at each subsequent level. Every country appoints its own markers who use a guide developed by the international contractor and the subject experts groups to mark the tests. Moderation is undertaken both locally and internationally. Scores are reported on a scale from 0 to 1,000 with a mean (average) set at 500 and a standard deviation of 100. The average score among OECD countries is 500 points. Approximately 66 per cent of students score between 400 and 600 points. The results offer a glimpse of how well those nearing the completion of their full-time secondary education have been prepared for adult life in participating countries.

Reflective Task

Can pupil achievements be compared across countries?

These surveys appear to offer an opportunity for countries to monitor and evaluate their teaching across time and across grades and provides an opportunity to examine performance of population subgroups, such as boys and girls, and address equity concerns using international data as a benchmark (Mullis *et al.*, 2005). TIMSS and PISA are very similar, providing different but, some argue, complementary information on student achievement in mathematics and science (Australian Government, 2008). There is, however, little connection between the two agencies that oversee them. In general terms, TIMSS seeks to find what students know and PISA seeks to find what students can do with their knowledge. Hutchinson and Schagen (2006) suggest that TIMSS inspects what is happening inside the classroom and PISA waits to see what comes out. TIMSS explores how well pupils in Year 8 have mastered the factual and procedural knowledge associated with mathematics and science. PISA concentrates on examining how well students are able to apply basic understandings and skills in reading, mathematics and science to everyday situations at the end of what is for most compulsory education. PISA also has a greater focus on data analysis, statistics and probability in mathematics. Detailed information on the cost of designing and administering the surveys is difficult to get hold of but it has been estimated that in 2003 TIMSS and PISA cost England £1 million to administer and deliver and the worldwide cost was well over £62 million (Prais, 2007).

In the light of what you have just read has your opinion changed since you undertook the Critical Thinking Task above? Why or why not? Reflect on your original answer.

Both surveys discussed in this chapter emphasise the need to take into account other factors when considering the raw data from the tests. Trying to capture the essence of secondary education in different countries is, in theory, given a high priority by the designers of TIMSS and PISA. In order to set the context for the next section some basic information about the differences between England and Finland, which have been chosen because comparison between the two raise some interesting questions about the viability of international surveys, are provided for you.

Table 4.1 Immediate points of comparison (OECD, 2007)

Country	Location	Area	Population	Population density	Expenditure on education per pupil
Finland	Scandinavia	338,145 sq km	5.3 million	15.5 per sq km	$7,402
England	Great Britain	130,281 sq km	50.4 million	386.9 per sq km	$7,290

Secondary education in England

The current form of secondary education in England originates in the 1944 Education (Butler) Act. This Act made secondary education free for all pupils and introduced the tripartite system which segregated schools into three distinct types, grammar, secondary modern and secondary technical. An examination at age 11 (known as the Eleven Plus) determined which one of these schools a pupil would attend. Later this system allowed for the creation of comprehensive schools which were a synthesis of the three different school types.

Secondary education is divided into two key stages (KS): KS3 for pupils aged 11 to 14 and KS4 for pupils aged 14 to 16. The majority of children are educated in non-selective 'maintained' schools supported financially by the state in one way or another (DCSF, 2007). Most are comprehensive in the sense that they accept pupils without taking academic ability into account, although a minority remain highly selective (e.g. grammar schools). Admissions criteria, where they apply, must be based on the mandatory School Admissions Code. Faith schools can give priority to those of an appropriate faith. Most pupils move from a primary school to a secondary school at age 11, (although in some areas of England a small number are educated in middle schools). Teaching is done mainly by subject specialist teachers to mixed ability classes, although there is some streaming in the core subjects of English, maths and science. Overall absenteeism is about 8.5 per cent. By far the majority of those not attending are in Year 11 at the end of KS4. In 2007, 24,000 (approximately 1 per cent) children left school without being entered for any public examinations at all and 153,000 (approximately 4.5 per cent) children left without a single 'C' grade (Lipsett, 2008).

The majority of publicly (state) funded secondary schools are mixed gender. Many also provide education for post-compulsory students aged 16 to 18+. The legal framework divides them into four principal types:

- Community Schools, managed and run by a local authority (LA) which employs staff, owns the land and school buildings and decides on admissions criteria.
- Foundation Schools, managed and run by a governing body. They usually own their own land and school buildings. A Trust School is a variant of a Foundation School in which a partnership is established with an outside agency such as a business or a charity.
- Voluntary Aided Schools, usually religious or faith-based. The governing body owns the land and school buildings, employs staff and makes a financial contribution (a minimum of 10 per cent) to its running costs.

- Voluntary Controlled Schools, similar to Voluntary Aided Schools in that they are owned by a charitable foundation but the LA employs staff and sets admissions policies.

Other state schools that cater for secondary pupils include:

- City Academies (CAs), established with substantial capital investment from business or voluntary, religious or private foundations to address a need for additional school places or as part of a wider school reorganisation. They can operate their own curriculum and pay their teachers more. The state pays the running costs.
- City Technology Colleges (CTCs) share many of the characteristics of CAs but concentrate on the teaching of science, mathematics and technology and offer a wide range of vocational qualifications in conjunction with those of a more traditional nature. Many are converting to CAs.
- Specialist Schools, including CAs, focus on a particular area such as business or the arts as well as teaching the curriculum as a whole.
- Pupil Referral Units (PRUs), which cater for children of compulsory school age who do not readily fit into the existing system for a variety of reasons. They concentrate on returning pupils back to the mainstream school.
- Special Schools for pupils with statutory statements of special educational needs.

A small but significant number of pupils are educated by the private sector in fee-paying, independent secondary schools that are not required to teach the National Curriculum but do generally work towards standard public examinations including the International Baccalaureate. Unlike the state sector they are not required to employ teachers with qualified teacher status (QTS) but must register with the Department for Children, Schools and Families (DCSF) and are subject to inspections.

The management of the secondary education system is undertaken at three different levels: national, local and institutional. The education service is overseen by the DCSF. It is responsible for administration, planning, and ensuring that provision is integrated. The system is inspected by OFSTED (Office for Standards in Education, Children's Services and Skills), a non-ministerial agency with a wide remit including children's services, schools, colleges, initial teacher training, youth work, work-based learning and adult education. The detailed organisation of publicly funded secondary education lies with 172 local authorities (LAs) in England. They have a responsibility for the maintenance of facilities, personnel issues, quality assurance and standards. They have also been required to integrate all children's and young people's services as a result of the Children's Act 2004 and Every Child Matters. All institutions have a governing body made up of mainly volunteer governors who have the collective legal responsibility of ensuring that the school maximises pupil achievement.

The school curriculum is overseen by the Qualifications and Curriculum Authority (QCA), a public body that advises the government on all curriculum issues. Schools are required to offer broad and balanced provision that meets the needs of all learners. Teaching methods and teaching materials are determined by the teacher. In England, the compulsory National Curriculum subjects for KS3 include:

- art and design;
- citizenship;
- design and technology (DT);
- English;
- geography;
- history;
- information and communication technology (ICT);
- mathematics;

- modern foreign language (MFL);
- music;
- physical education (PE);
- religious education (RE);
- science.

At KS4 the subjects pupils are required to study include citizenship, English, ICT, mathematics, RE, science and PE. They can also choose to undertake a range of other subjects (usually selected from those available at KS3). In addition, sex and careers education are compulsory in both KS3 and KS4, as is work-related learning (usually involving a placement in an out-of-school setting) in KS4. Schools are also expected, but not obliged, to provide personal, social and health education (PSHE) throughout all key stages. Most subject-related study leads to standard public exams, such as the General Certificate of Secondary Education (GCSE) at the end of KS4 and Advanced (A) levels for pupils during KS5. In the move to personalise learning for all children the Special Educational Needs and Disability Act 2001 increased the rights of SEN pupils to be educated alongside their mainstream peers. Secondary school teachers are not civil servants. They are employed either by a LA or an individual school. In maintained schools they are obliged to have Qualified Teacher Status (QTS) which has been obtained as a result of successfully completing a teaching related programme, either at undergraduate or postgraduate level, as explained in Chapter Six.

Secondary education in Finland

Until the 1960s pupils in Finland were divided into two parallel streams at the age of ten, based on academic ability, allowing the most able pupils to pursue higher education while others followed a strictly vocational route. The foundation for the current system was laid down by the 1968 Act on Schools. This had equality and comprehensive education at its heart – it was designed to integrate an educationally divided nation. However, schooling:

. . .was also bitterly criticized by politicians, media and many parents, too. The opponents argued that the common comprehensive school would lower academic expectations and hence gradually lead to poorer educational attainment, especially among more able and talented pupils.

Sahlberg, 2006, page 4

There are almost 3,500 comprehensive schools (Peruskoulu or Grundskola) catering for nearly 600,000 pupils (Ministry of Education, 2007a). They vary in the age groups they embrace, catering for one of the following ranges:

- primary pupils (ages 7–13);
- lower secondary pupils (ages 13–16);
- all compulsory sector pupils (ages 7–16).

They vary in the size of their intake – by far the greatest majority have more than 100 and less than 500 pupils in them. There are no single sex schools. Finnish is the dominant language in most (nearly 3,200 schools) but there are some that provide for mainly Swedish-speaking pupils (315) and those with other mother tongues (7). Schools can be maintained by municipalities or private organisations and foundations, subject to government approval. Special schools also exist that cater for those with recognised disabilities (over 10,000 pupils) such as visual impairment.

Secondary education in Finland consists of compulsory lower secondary level (ages 13–16, grades 7 to 9) and non-compulsory upper secondary level (ages 16–18 or 19, grades 10 to 12).

The term secondary as applied in the English sense does not readily translate to a Finnish context. Children in the KS3 and KS4 age range are part of what the Finnish regard as a nine year basic education cycle that stretches from ages 7–16. There is some separation between primary (7–13) and lower secondary (13–16) sectors in that instruction in the first six years is usually undertaken by the class teacher and then specialists in the remaining years. The vast majority of pupils are taught in non-selective comprehensive (basic) schools maintained by local municipalities (councils) and funded by the state. There are no admissions criteria and transition between pre-upper secondary stages is guaranteed. Students are not streamed according to ability. It is compulsory for 13–16-year-olds to complete the requisite syllabus but they are not obliged to attend school to do so. However, the child's guardian is responsible for ensuring that it is met. A certificate, which is a necessary requirement for transition to all upper secondary education, is issued on completion of the syllabus. Dropping out of school and repeating years are rare. Almost all children (99.7 per cent) obtain the necessary certificate to continue their education to age 18. Equal educational opportunities are at the heart of the Finnish system which is designed to support *the development of pupils as human beings, and their growth into ethically responsible members of society, and the promotion of learning and equality in society*. The cost of teaching, learning materials, school meals, health care, dental care and school transport are met by the state.

On completion of basic education at age 16 pupils have a number of different options:

• Study at a general upper secondary school (*Lukio* or *Gymnasium*) for three years preparing for the national matriculation examination leading to higher education. Some specialise in one particular area such as music, physical education, the fine arts, languages or natural sciences.
• Train for three years at a vocational upper-secondary school in preparation for almost any occupational area. This also can lead to higher education.
• Engage in other post-compulsory education or training (such as apprenticeship training).
• Undertake a voluntary additional 10th grade of basic school.
• Employment.

Education nationally is overseen centrally by the Ministry of Education and the Finnish National Board of Education (FNBE). The ministry is responsible for schools, higher education, educational research and drafting and submitting educational legislation to the government. It also decides on the level of government funding for individual institutions. The FNBE, which was established in 1991, is responsible for developing aims, curriculum and methodology for primary, lower and upper and vocational secondary and further education. It also helps to develop national educational policy, establish national criteria for pupil assessment and evaluate educational outcomes on behalf of the ministry. Education locally is overseen authorities (LMAs) which have tax raising powers and are obliged by law to provide comprehensive education for all children living within their boundaries. Six State Provincial Offices monitor and evaluate LMAs on behalf of the Ministry.

The national core curriculum (NCC) for basic education is taught to pupils in both mainstream and special education between the ages of 7–16. Established by the National Board of Education in January 2004, it is composed of:

• arts (visual art, craft, music);
• environmental studies and geography;
• health education and home economics;
• history and social studies;
• languages (Finnish, Romany, Swedish or Sami language and literature depending on the mother tongue of the individual, plus Finnish or Swedish as a second language and modern foreign languages);

- mathematics;
- physical education (PE);
- religion or ethics;
- science (biology, chemistry, physics).

Optional subjects, particularly with an arts or skill base, can be taught too. There are also a number of cross-curricular themes in the NCC including growth as a person, cultural identity and internationalism, media skills and communication, participatory citizenship and entre-preneurship, responsibility for the environment, well-being and sustainable future, safety and traffic and technology and the individual. An LMA or school-specific curriculum based on the NCC can be created by education providers to better reflect local conditions. There are private schools in Finland but they are funded by the state, publicly supervised and obliged to follow national core curriculum.

Unlike their English counterparts teachers are civil servants employed by the LMA. The majority in basic schools are women. All teachers require a Masters level education degree, including their specialist subject for subject teachers. Teachers are not obligated to be at school on days when they are not teaching or engaged in other school-related duties.

Critical Thinking Task

Norms and values

Functional theory developed by early social philosophers such as Comte and Durkheim and refined and extended by Parsons claims that society is an interconnected network of related agencies which seek equilibrium (Slattery, 2003). Parsons believed that in order for a society to survive the component parts, including education, must work towards the common good by promoting shared norms and values.

Identify the norms and values indicated by the secondary education system in England and Finland. Start the exercise by identifying the similarities and differences between the two systems. For example:

- What is the function of education as expressed through the secondary system in each of the two countries?
- How are pupils seen – as individuals or components of a class or year group?
- Are teachers in England and Finland educated to the same level? What is the difference?
- What might the level of teacher education say about the value placed on education or the respect shown to teachers by society?

2006 survey results

Although England has participated in a number of TIMSS surveys, Finland has not. This means that the only point of meaningful comparison between the two countries is by using PISA data, from the most recent survey in 2006 which focused on science.

England (Science) had an average of 516 point score in science and was ranked fourteenth. Only seven countries had mean scores which were higher, thirteen had similar mean scores and thirty-six had lower mean scores. It had the third highest proportion of students reaching Level 6 with only New Zealand and Finland better. It had a wider spread of attainment when compared with many other countries. As well as high achievers, it also had a substantial number of low-scoring students.

Finland (Science) had an average of 563 point score in science and was ranked first. The number of Finnish students reaching Level 6 was three times the OECD average, with over one in five reaching at least Level 5. The differences between the performance of the weakest and strongest in Finland were amongst the smallest in the survey. The differences in performance between schools, regions, pupils from different socio-economic background and the various language groups are also remarkably small. It appears that all schools deliver consistently high-quality science education regardless of type, size or location (Ministry of Education, 2007b).

Summary of PISA results

The following tables show England's and Finland's placing based on PISA results when all participating countries are ranked in order of achievement.

Table 4.2

England	Mathematics	Reading	Science
2000	8th	7th	4th
2003	No meaningful data for international comparison		
2006	24th	17th	14th

Table 4.3

Finland	Mathematics	Reading	Science
2000	4th	1st	3rd
2003	2nd	1st	3rd
2006	2nd	2nd	1st

When viewed in conjunction with performance in previous surveys the 2006 results, imply that Finland has maintained its pre-eminent position whilst England appears to have slipped inexorably down the league table in all of three subject areas tested. This was the conclusion that the headline writers came to despite the caution from the OECD that results are not directly comparable between different surveys because the number of countries participating and the nature of the tests varied between surveys. An article which announced that the UK plummeted in the world rankings for maths and reading appeared in the Education Guardian in a direct response to the survey (Lipsett, 2007). It led to the Director of the Royal Society (the UK's national academy of science) asking how the UK can be expected to compete economically in the future if:

. . . all our young people are not as well educated as those in other countries? Science and mathematics are essential to our future economic wellbeing, yet we are seeing the UK stumble down the world rankings in these subjects. We must now look to see why this has happened and do what is necessary to put it right.

Lipsett, 2007

On the other hand, the Finns quietly celebrated their apparent pre-eminence, using their performance in the PISA surveys to promote external investment in Finland. Pehkonen *et al.*, (2007) who were as surprised as many others by the 2000 and 2003 results, believe that there are many factors that have led to this success, but they identify three in particular.

- Research culture in teacher education.
- School and curriculum.
- The use of ICT.

The Finnish Ministry of Education attributed the success not only to egalitarianism but a very cost-effective education system. The country's President commentated that besides having a free system open to all, the notion that education is a good thing is deeply ingrained in Finnish culture. She states that it is greatly *appreciated and there is a broad political consensus on education policy* (Halonen, 2008).

Practical Task |

Improvements for secondary education

This chapter has given you an overview of both the English and Finnish secondary education systems and their relative PISA ranking.

- Working in a group, make a list of some priorities each government might adopt in order to improve their secondary education. For example, England might wish to review education or training beyond the age of 16. Finland might wish to reconsider basic and in-service training of teachers.
- Use the norms and values you identified in the previous task to help you rank the priorities for each country.
- Once you have come up with your group list you can compare your thoughts with the priorities identified by each government. These can be found on the following websites:
  – England: **www.dcsf.gov.uk/index.htm**
  – Finland: **www.oph.fi/english/pageLast.asp?path=447,4699,4762**
- Given that Finland achieved so highly in the PISA survey what reasons do you think the government might have for not taking part in TIMMS? Make a list of the possibilities.
- Using the PISA and TIMMS Websites look at the survey results for a country of your choice. Each member of the group should choose a different country. How does your country compare to England and Finland and to those selected by your group members? What might be the reasons for its higher or lower achievement?

Perspectives on international surveys

This examination of the use of surveys to measure performance of secondary education systems in different countries inevitably raises more questions than answers. Some argue that international league tables are as unreliable as domestic ones, asserting that they do not compare like with like. Dunn and Goddard (2002) believe that the actual rankings may not be as meaningful as some groups would like them to be. If there are (statistically) significant differences in PISA scores between countries they should not be assumed to result solely from variations in schooling but rather from the cumulative effect of learning taking pace both in and outside school. At best, the surveys only represent an estimate of the performance of the target populations because of the use of sampling. Statistics cannot meaningfully take account of variations in different groups with complete accuracy and therefore errors can be included. There are mathematical techniques that can be employed to measure how good the estimate is but some form of inaccuracy is implicit. Sets of results with very small differences are particularly meaningless because they cannot be relied upon to be repeated consistently if exactly the same exercise is undertaken again. The only way to ensure complete reliability is if every pupil, rather than a few, took the relevant test. Participation varies both across surveys and within countries rendering the examination of results over time to establish trends more problematic. In 2003, England was excluded from both TIMMS and PISA for failing to meet the benchmark response rate despite a large investment by the government in collection methods. Figures for the whole of the UK were presented but these were not deemed suitable for international comparison. More fundamentally, Smithers (2004) argues that some surveys have less to say about the performance of education systems than they would like to think they have because they are inherently flawed. He cites PISA in particular, with its concentration on outcome rather than curriculum, as one example of this.

The best international educational surveys make a great effort to assure participants that the most stringent checking procedures are used in relationship to data collection and marking of scripts to assure parity between countries. The reality is that it is extremely difficult to do this. A newspaper editorial referring to the 2006 PISA results in England declared that despite great care on the part of the OECD:

. . . monitoring systems differ widely in the 57 countries covered. Each of the 57, moreover, has its own circumstances within which education operates. Improvements in countries which have languished due to poverty, disorder, oppression – or merely because of bad government – will push a nation up the ladder, without necessarily meaning that others are thereby in crisis.

The *Guardian* editorial, 2007

Even if consensus is reached about the value of the results they can mean different things to different groups. In Finland, Rautalin and Alasuutari (2007) writing from the perspective of teacher unions about the 2006 PISA survey, made reference to what they called the curse of success hiding the real issues in Finnish education. They state that despite the league position basic education is gravely under-resourced, the school network in Finland is deteriorating and the education sector does not receive as much attention or appreciation as it does in other OECD countries. Whilst in England the general secretary of the National Union of Teachers declared that he was unconvinced that comparison between 2000 and 2006 PISA surveys indicated decline or that teaching was unsatisfactory. He said that more science teachers were needed and questioned the value of an over-prescribed and overloaded science curriculum (Lipsett, 2007).

By far the most perplexing element of the survey conundrum is how you take into account the cultural factors in any evaluation. Culture in this sense is not just about mores or habits – it is more fundamental. Grønmol et al. (2004) point out that there are distinct customs in mathematics and science. There is a Nordic, an English-speaking, a German-speaking, an East Asian and an East European tradition that need to be accounted. Factors such as geography and political history are influential when curricula are set up and textbooks written. Purves (1987) suggests that in order to understand why students in a particular system of education perform as they do '. . . *one must often reach deep into the cultural and educational history of that system and education.*' This is what comparative education seeks to do.

Chapter Summary

This chapter has discussed secondary education in England and Finland with reference to international education assessment surveys.

- International assessment surveys are undertaken by a variety of agencies and are of particular interest to government, journalists and educators as a way of comparing their country's educational performance with others.
- Three of the most popular surveys are TIMMS, PISA and PIRLS.
- Secondary education (and the pupil opportunities it leads on to), as with other levels of education, is strongly influenced by the values and culture of the country.
- Cultural differences make it very difficult to actually compare countries' results in international surveys and we should be cautious when making such comparisons.

Research focus

Task 1

A seminal text on international assessment surveys is:

- Moskowitz, JH and Stephens, M (2004) *Comparing learning outcomes: International assessment and education policy.* Abingdon: Routledge Falmer.

It discusses in detail the usefulness of education assessment data, the political importance and public interest and explores key issues related to these vast assessment programmes:

The ten chapters are produced as a collaborative effort by a group of countries that have been working together for over ten years in an OECD project that collects and publishes cross-national comparative information on education for use by governments.

Moskowitz and Stephens, page 1

As such it is written by a group of comparative educationalists and is a useful read to extend your knowledge and understanding on the themes of this chapter. Read it and make careful notes.

Task 2

A useful research task to undertake is to look at PISA data for Wales, Scotland and Northern Ireland. They can be found as below:

- Scotland, **www.scotland.gov.uk/Resource/Doc/205528/0054694.pdf**
- Wales, **http://new.wales.gov.uk/topics/educationandskills/publications/reports/pisa2006? lang=en**
- Northern Ireland, **http://new.wales.gov.uk/topics/educationandskills/publications/reports/ pisa2006?lang=en**

Look at the data and compare it to that of England.

Task 3

An excellent article showing how TIMMS has been used to compare and contrast curricula is:

• Murdock, J (2008) Comparison of curricular breadth, depth, and recurrence and physics achievement of TIMMS population 3 countries. *International Journal of Science Education,* 30 (9): 1135–1157

Read this paper to try and understand how the data were used to reach the conclusions proposed.

References

Australian Government (2008) *Why TIMSS and PISA?* (online) Available at: **www.dest.gov.au/ sectors/school_education/publications_resources/schooling_issues_digest/perf_aus_ schools/why.htm** (accessed 30 November 2008).

BBC (2007) *England falls in Reading League.* Available at: **http://news.bbc.co.uk/1/hi/ education/7117230.stm** (accessed 19th January 2009).

Curtis, P (2007) UK falls to 14th place in science teaching table. The Guardian, 29/11/07 (online). Available at: **www.guardian.co.uk/education/2007/nov/29/schools.uk1** (accessed 15 November 2008).

Department for Children, Schools and Families (2007) *National statistics: schools and pupils in England, January 2007, National Statistics, SFR30/2007* (online). Available at: **www.dcsf.gov.uk/rsgateway/DB/SFR/s000744/UPDATEDSFR30_2007.pdf** (accessed 30 November 2008).

Document Summary Service (2007) *Achievements of 15 year olds in England, OECD/PISA 2006 national report, a summary of the NFER report, December 2007.* Bristol: University of Bristol.

Dunn, M and Goddard, E (2002) *Student achievement in England: results in reading, mathematical and scientific literacy among 15-year-olds from OECD PISA 2000 study.* London: The Stationery Office.

Grønmo, L, Kjærnsli, M and Lie, S (2004) Looking for cultural and geographical factors in patterns of responses to TIMSS items. *International Research Conference Proceedings,* 99–112. Cyprus: Cyprus University Press.

Guardian Editorial, (2007) The truth about the tables. The *Guardian,* 07/12/07 (online). Available at: **www.guardian.co.uk/commentisfree/2007/dec/06/schools.publicservices** (accessed 26 September 2008).

Gurria, A (2007) PISA, *The OECD programme for international student assessment.* Paris: OECD.

Halonen, T (2008) *Address by President of the Republic Tarja Halonen* at the University of Minnesota, Duluth Honorary Degree Ceremony in Duluth, 25/07/08.

Hegarty, S. (2004) How countries can profit from participating in TIMMS, *Significance of TIMMS,* Press Packet Statement, 14/12/04 (online). Available at: **http://timss.bc.edu/timss 2003i/conference_IR.html#presskit** (accessed 30 November 2008).

Hutchinson, D and Scagen, I (2006) *Comparisons between PISA and TIMMS: Are we the man with two watches,* National Foundation for Educational Research, presented at IEA Second International Research Conference, Washington, 9–11 November 2006 (online). Available at: **www.brookings.edu/gs/brown/irc2006conference/HutchisonSchagen_presentation. pdf** (30 September 2008).

IES National Centre for Education Statistics (2008) *Education indicators: An international perspective* (online) Available at: **http://nces.ed.gov/surveys/international/intlindicators/** (accessed 16 November 2008).

Lipsett, A (2007) Because the number of countries participating and the nature of the tests has varied, The *Guardian*, 04/12/07(online). Available at: **www.guardian.co.uk/education/2007/dec/04/schools.uk2** (15 November 2008).

Lipsett, A (2008) Tories claim millions leave school without good GCSEs, The *Guardian*, 20/08/08 (online). Available at: **www.guardian.co.uk/education/2008/aug/20/lackof qualifications** (15 November 2008).

Ministry of Education (2007a) *Improving school leadership, Finland*. Helsinki: Ministry of Finland.

Ministry of Education,(2007b) *Finland's success in the PISA survey.* Helsinki: Ministry of Finland.

Mullis, I, Martin, M, Ruddock, O'Sullivan, Arora, A and Erberber, E (2007) *Timms 2007 assessment framework*. Boston: TIMMS & PIRLS International Study Centre.

OECD (2007) *PISA 2006 science competencies for tomorrow's world, executive summary*. Paris: OECD.

Pehkonen, E, Ahtee, M and Lavonen (2007) Explanations for the Finnish success in PISA evaluations. *Proceedings of the 29th annual meeting of the North American Chapter of the International Group for the Psychology of Mathematics Education*, University of Nevada, Reno, 2007.

Prais, SJ (2007) Two recent international surveys of schooling attainments in mathematics: England's problems. *Oxford Review of Education*, 33(1): 33–46.

Purves, A (1987) IEA agenda for the future. *International Review of Education*, 33: 103–107.

Rautalin, M and Alasuutari, P (2007) The curse of success: the impact of the OECD's Programme for International Students. *European Educational Research Journal,* 6(4): 348–63

Sahlberg, P (2006) Raising the bar: How Finland responds to the twin challenge of secondary education? *Profesorado, Revista de curriculum y formacion del profesorado,* 10(1) (2006) (online). Available at: **www.ugr.es/~recfpro/rev101ART4ing.pdf** (accessed 19 November 2008)

Slattery, M (2003) *Key ideas in sociology.* London: Nelson Thornes.

Smithers, A (2004) True to form. The *Guardian*, 14/12/04 (online). Available at: **www.guardian. co.uk/education/2004/dec/14/teaching.politics** (accessed 19 November 2008).

Chapter 5

Money and massification: international issues in higher education

Wendy Bignold and Liz Gayton

Learning outcomes

By the end of this chapter you should be able to:

- debate the purpose of higher education, voicing your own informed views;
- recognise how national governments influence or control universities and the importance of the political context to higher education;
- understand the key issues facing British universities in the twenty-first century and how these issues relate to some other countries and investigate how they affect countries not discussed here;
- provide a critical analysis of some different ways by which higher education has attempted to address these issues in Great Britain and elsewhere.

Chapter outline

Universities have always prompted as much debate about themselves and the nature of what they do as they have stimulated on their campuses in the pursuit of new knowledge. This continues to be the case today both within and across different countries. This chapter examines four major issues faced by higher education institutions around the world. Starting with Britain, it takes these four areas from the Dearing Report (1997) which has had a major impact on British higher education, setting out, as it did, recommendations to the government about the development of *higher education in the learning society* (Dearing, 1997). The four major areas identified in the report for particular attention from the government and universities are:

- issues relating to funding;
- expansion and widening participation;
- the professionalisation of academic staff;
- the continued assurance of world-class standards.

Concerns in these areas have been felt by academics around the world and comparisons are made to several other countries, particularly to India, China and the United States. These four issues will be discussed in turn before considering the purpose of higher education and student experience. Higher education institutions around the world include both universities and colleges of higher education, and this chapter combines both.

The three countries selected for particular attention here, alongside Britain, have each been chosen for different reasons. Higher education in India is undergoing rapid expansion, and massification, in an attempt to ensure a far greater percentage of the population are able to attend college or university in a move to benefit both individuals and the state. China too is experiencing massification of its higher education provision but particularly interesting is its move away from tight government control under the rigid communist policies of the mid- and late 1900s to a system which is based far more on western universities. The USA is selected here as it is so often perceived to provide quality services, including education, given its assumed place as the dominant world power. However, like most countries, it has its own internal issues which it is seeking to address and this is also true of higher education there.

The funding debate

Funding of higher education – who pays for it? – has long been an issue in many countries. This is a contentious matter as only a minority of the population directly participate; in Britain this is approximately 40 per cent.

England has seen a significant change in higher education funding in recent years with the introduction of variable tuition fees for students. Previously the state subsidised higher education for many students, depending on their family's financial income. Prior to 2006, tuition fees were set at the same amount for all institutions. Now individual universities can choose how much students should pay for tuition (to attend). Increasingly fierce competition for students has led to some institutions lowering their fees to attract more of them. Welsh students are effectively exempt from top-up fees if they stay in Wales because they receive a non-means-tested grant from the Welsh government. In Scotland, students have to make no personal contribution to fees except when studying for a second degree or postgraduate award. Alongside tuition fees from students, each institution receives a grant from the Higher Education Funding Council of England, the Higher Education Funding Council for Wales or the Scottish Higher Education Funding Council, based on the number of students registered. Those offering professional courses also receive grants from the relevant professional funding bodies, (for example, teacher-training degrees are funded by the Teacher Development Agency).

Reflective Task

Who should pay for higher education?

There is an ongoing debate as to who should pay for higher education. Some argue that it benefits society as a whole with a workforce that has an enhanced level of knowledge and skills and therefore it should be publicly funded. Others believe that it is those who go to university who should pay the costs as they will benefit directly, generally entering graduate employment with a higher salary than those who do not have a degree. Consider each of the questions below and reflect carefully before you answer.

1. How do each of those listed below benefit from higher education and to what extent?
 • students and their families; local communities where students live or work on graduation; future employers;
 • the government; society generally (the state).

2. Who, then, do you think should pay for higher education?

3. Should who pays for higher education depend on what subject is studied? For example, do you think society benefits more from a graduate who studied to become a teacher or from a graduate who studied Ancient Greek? What about a mature student who has

retired and chooses to study at university as part of his or her leisure activities out of interest? Is this different to a young student who is studying for a future career?

4. If students pay for higher education, do they become 'customers' of the universities? Does higher education then become a product? What might be the implications of this for (a) the university; and (b) the student?

The Dearing Report recommended that in Britain *students enter into an obligation to make contributions to the cost of their education once they are in work*. This was taken up by the British government who, rather than opting for a 'graduate tax' approach, decided that most students in England would pay a tuition fee at the beginning of their course. This was later modified so that the government paid the fee up-front as a 'student loan', with the student paying back after graduation. Changes in funding arrangements in England have required many students to take on additional paid employment which can have a negative impact on their learning (Beaumont, 2007).

Governments around the world have addressed funding in various ways. Scandinavian countries took the decision that the benefits to individuals and the whole of society justified the investment of large amounts of tax payers' money in their higher education provision. So students have to pay little apart from their living expenses. Australia, Japan, Korea and New Zealand are amongst countries that, whilst also using tax payers' money, have shifted some of the costs on to students (OECD, 2007). Many European countries, on the other hand, have opted not to increase public investment in their universities or to allow them to charge tuition fees. As a result of this, the amount of money spent on each student in many European universities is less than fifty per cent of spending in American institutions. The British government (DfES, 2003) acknowledges that funding for higher education in England has for a long time been lower than in other European countries, including France, Germany and the Netherlands, and considerably lower than in the United States. In comparison, Japan's investment in higher education is planned to exceed that of England in the near future.

Indian universities and colleges of higher education have been funded by the State with the University Grant Commission (UGC) paying a set amount to individual institutions towards their running costs, including staff salaries, regardless of the number of students enrolled at each institution. This position is changing now with the national government gradually withdrawing funding. Currently the UGC funds 80 per cent with the remaining 20 per cent coming from the regional state governments at a local level. As a result of this funding model student fees have been very low and, to a large extent, still are. Many Indian academics regard low student fees as a disadvantage because they require little financial investment from many students and this can lead to low levels of motivation and commitment. Applied courses, such as Business Management Studies or Environmental Science, can charge higher fees. They still remain popular with students despite their higher costs as they provide a better chance of employment on graduation. But such a system of variable fees throws up issues of equality of opportunity for students from low socio-economic groups who cannot afford higher fees.

There is a global trend then, in higher education, for more and more students to rely on grants and loans in order to attain a degree, resulting in substantial debt upon graduation. Higher education in China used to be funded by the government only. However, changes over the last ten years now allow universities to seek funding from a variety of other sources including, primarily, students' tuition fees, external research funding and enterprise activities, mirroring trends in Britain, India and elsewhere.

The shift away from full government funding to an increase in student financial contributions and external funding in Britain and India has been replicated in many other countries. All three sources currently provide funding for higher education in the USA, with more and more burden placed on students and their families as governmental budgets are strained. Scholarship money is still available, but even those sources are under financial attack. Recently some elite American universities promised larger financial aid packages up to and including a totally free four-year degree programme. How effective these attempts are to ameliorate the rising costs of higher education for middle and lower income families has not been yet tested. American institutions today regularly measure their 'discount rate', that is, the percentage of tuition charges that is rebated to students in the form of scholarships, loans, work/study awards, or other forms of financial aid. It seems that, as costs rise, institutions themselves find ways to make higher education seem more affordable to students and their families. There is greater differentiation of funding sources in the USA than in Britain, with state-funded colleges and universities receiving direct tax dollars, and independent, private, and religiously affiliated institutions relying mainly on endowments, donations, tuition and other funding, but also receiving state and federal monies in a variety of schemes.

Historical *Perspective*

Changing levels of government influence on universities

In recent times some British universities have had a high level of autonomy. However, this is diminishing as many universities are heavily reliant on government funding, despite the introduction of student fees and research funding from external bodies. For this reason, universities (some more than others) have to address issues at the top of the government's agenda if they wish to secure additional government grants for achieving policy targets. This subtle shift in the level of government 'control' puts some universities in a new historical era of reduced autonomy and independence.

In India the government is increasing its influence and hold over universities as it controls significant amounts of funding. This brings with it various criteria that universities and affiliated colleges must adhere to in order to access funds and in so doing they are obliged to comply with government expectations. It was not always like this, as the ancient Indian traditions demonstrate. The first millennium and the few centuries preceding it saw the flourishing of higher education at Nalanda, Takshashila, Ujjain and Vikramshila universities in India. Art, architecture, painting, logic, mathematics, grammar, philosophy, astronomy, literature, Buddhism, Hinduism, economics and politics, law and medicine were among the early disciplines taught and each university specialised in a particular field of study. In these early days of higher education the emphasis was very much on philosophy and the philosophy of each subject – philosophical debate was a major tradition in ancient Indian universities. However, at the start of the second millennium, universities are required to address the vocational needs of society and students, with an increased emphasis on knowledge and skills, in order to access government funding.

Interestingly China is reversing this trend of increased government influence. In the late 1800s, China developed a higher education system based on the western university model. With the founding of the People's Republic of China, a communist country, the central government dominated every aspect of life from the 1950s onwards, including higher education provision as the Soviet Union model was adopted (Duan, 2003). There was a complete lack of autonomy for universities, which resulted in low institutional efficiency due to a lack of motivation in academics tied to tight government controls. The 1990s to the present day has seen a transfer of administrative power to local government which is increasing institutions' involvement in their development. This historical perspective is tightly influenced then by a changing political perspective as the Communist Party of China modernises.

American universities have a reputation for being places of liberal and radical biases and views, suggesting anti-government and establishment stances (Smith *et al.*, 2008). A recent survey of the top 64 doctoral research institutions found this not to be so, suggesting a stronger level of government influence than expected. Of course, as with the other countries discussed, funding is tightly controlled by the government in the USA and so it is impossible for universities not to be influenced by the government.

Expansion and widening participation

At the beginning of the twenty-first century, the British government is committed to getting 50 per cent of young adults into higher education. To successfully meet this target, an increasingly diverse range of students will have to be recruited.

Critical Thinking Task

Who should go to university?

Read the following information and answer the questions.

Education in the twenty-first century is undergoing significant change at all levels with an increased focus on inclusion of all pupils and students. Inclusive education is well illustrated by Barton who describes it thus:

Inclusive education is part of a human rights approach to social relations and conditions. The intentions and values involved relate to a vision of the whole society of which education is a part. Issues of social justice, equity and choice are central to demands for inclusive education.

Barton, 2003, page 59

1. What do you understand is meant by the term 'social justice'?

There is a long tradition in many countries of the children of the middle classes and wealthy elite attending university at the exclusion of those from low-income families. This is particularly so in countries operating a capitalist economy. Consider the questions below, analysing in your own mind how the political context of a country might impact on its colleges of higher education and universities.

2. What might you expect participation trends to be in communist countries and why would this be so?
3. How does a country's political system influence participation trends in higher education? How might higher education provision differ between a communist country and a capitalist country, for example?
4. Should everyone have the opportunity to attend higher education? Can everyone benefit from it? Should only those who can afford to pay for it be allowed to attend? Try to justify your reasoning.

The importance of widening participation depends on the perspective taken and the viewpoint within that. A philosophical perspective on widening participation is that it is promotes social justice. It is a human right to have access to education and this includes higher education for those who want it. Such a view would favour an inclusive education system of lifelong learning opportunities underpinned by values which promote equity and choice for individuals and groups (Barton, 2003). A sociological perspective would be one where higher education is seen as benefiting the whole of society as more people have high-level skills needed to secure economic growth for the country. There is also evidence that graduates are more likely to be engaged citizens, making a positive contribution to their communities (DfES, 2003).

The term 'social justice' has been reintroduced into British politics and higher education and like other sectors of society this is expected to be driven by *principles of economic redistribution, social inclusion and moral responsibility* (Riddell, 2005). Widening participation and fair access means increased opportunities for people from under-represented groups to participate successfully in all aspects of higher education (e.g. low socio-economic groups and minority ethnic groups), including those offering the highest financial returns in graduate employment. In England and Wales there has been a gradual progress in broadening the socio-economic make-up of the student population, but progress has been slow and evidence suggests that it may be levelling off (DfES, 2006). Scottish universities have been doing rather better with approximately 53 per cent of cohorts there being drawn from under-represented groups. Universities in England, Wales and Scotland have undertaken activities to promote widening participation under four broad headings:

* raising attainment in primary and secondary education;
* raising aspirations;
* encouraging applications; reviewing admissions procedures.

The British government's commitment to expanding participation is partly based on research which shows that the economy will require an increase in people with higher-level skills (DfES, 2003). The UK economy is increasingly knowledge-based with livings being made through selling high-value services rather than physical goods. Despite this, government evidence suggests that many of the increased jobs will be in associate professional and high-level technician jobs which do not necessarily require a traditional three-year honours degree. Two-year, employment-related foundation degrees are one example of a strategic approach to ensuring that courses and patterns of study on offer not only match the needs of the economy but provide alternative routes to higher education qualifications for a more diverse range of students.

Education in India is valued by the family as it is seen as a way to improve quality of life, as one of the paths to upward social mobility. As competition to secure well-paid jobs increases so the required level of qualification for that job rises, and higher education degrees are becoming an increasingly common requirement. Despite giving opportunities to support under-represented groups of students through scholarships or, more recently, bank loans at very low interest rates, the education system in India currently represents a great paradox. On the one hand, it has International Institutes of Management and International Institutes of Technology that rank among the best higher education institutions in the world and, on the other hand, there are still schools in the country that do not even have the basic infrastructure for primary education. Fifty years after independence from Britain and the establishment of the modern Indian state, the country is still far away from its goal of universal literacy despite steps forward to widen participation in higher education:

Thus, India has to find a strategy that will enable it to effectively address the multiple challenges in the education sector of improving literacy, universalising access to quality basic and secondary education and at the same time ensuring an adequate supply of higher skills and technically trained manpower.

Kaul, 2006, page 5

This is a key issue which India is addressing and which is driving, in part, government policy on higher education expansion.

Expansion of higher education has been a major issue for China too with the government setting an increased target of 25 per cent more students by 2010, a total target of 16 million students. It has rapidly increased the number of places available by increasing the number of colleges and universities:

China is now the largest higher education system in the world: it awards more university degrees than the US and India combined. Of course, this is partly a matter of the sheer size of its population. But it is not just that. The rate of university expansion has been beyond anything anyone in the West can easily imagine. University enrolments in China have reportedly risen from under 10% of young people in 1999 to over 21% in 2006, a phenomenally fast expansion.

Baker, 2007

It has also started to address widening participation with a focus on domestic migrant workers' children (Law, 2006), amongst others. This low-economic income group have traditionally been excluded from post-compulsory education, including higher education. As their parents, or they themselves, move around the country following work opportunities they fall foul of educational administrative regulations at a local level. Differing curricula studied in different areas and lack of entitlement to junior graduation certificates if away from their place of origin make it difficult to gain the necessary educational qualifications to secure a university place. Like the UK government, the Chinese government is recognising the value of widening participation and groups such as this one, which have traditionally been excluded, are increasingly the focus of new initiatives aimed at meeting their particular needs, such as scholarships for students from under-represented groups.

The US government has a focus on increasing the number of higher education graduates in society who can fully participate in, and contribute to the new global economy. While the number of American students attending higher education institutions has increased over the last few decades, there is concern that the financial issues discussed earlier may affect that trend. One strategy for expansion has been to review the role of so-called community colleges (two-year courses) which provide preparation in basic academics, but which also focus on vocational and technical training. Students wishing to pursue a four-year degree would traditionally begin at such an institution, and then transfer to another institution to attain a four-year bachelor's degree. These community colleges are now lobbying for the right to issue four-year degrees, thus increasing the number of student places in higher education. One component of the debate is whether simply having the degree is as important as having substance behind it – many believe the community colleges are not up to this task and would be hard put to staff the necessary changes. This illustrates a potential issue in the expansion of higher education faced by any country – how can you increase quantity (expand) and maintain quality, particularly with the global trend for reduced government funding?

In other ways, broadened participation and student diversity in higher education is a huge political issue in the USA at the moment and has more often been taken to mean 'racial and ethnic' diversity rather than economic or social diversity. Politicians of every sort are promoting discussions and initiatives for raising the number of residents who attain a higher education degree. In the last half of the twentieth century, American institutions, through a variety of schemes, weighted the applications of students from minority ethnic backgrounds in order to accept a fixed proportion of such students in each year's incoming class. These so-called 'affirmative action' practices were challenged in court and have been generally disallowed. In comparison some institutions in India have held on to their quota admission targets in order to address inequality of access to higher education.

Professionalisation of academic staff

In most universities in Britain the qualification required to become a lecturer is a higher degree, as in a masters or, increasingly, a doctorate. There is no requirement to have any formal teaching qualification unless training teachers themselves. As a result of this there was wide-spread concern that new lecturers may be proficient in research but not in the pedagogical aspects of their subject. The Dearing Report recommended the establishment of an Institute for Learning and Teaching in Higher Education (ILT) which would, amongst other things, accredit academics in teaching. Dearing also recommended that new teaching staff should attain membership of the ILT, usually by completing an accredited certificate in Learning and Teaching. Recognising the paramount importance of excellent support of student learning, many universities across Britain now require their staff to complete such a qualification, thus increasing the professionalism of academics.

In India, universities have, for a long time, generally required doctorates of their academic staff. In a bid to raise standards across the whole of the higher education sector there, their affiliated colleges now have similar expectations of all tutors. Private colleges, of which there are increasing numbers due to increasing student demand, do not have this requirement and as such the quality of education they offer may arguably not be so high. However, they will continue to recruit students by charging lower fees than the government-affiliated universities and colleges. This throws up issues of comparability and equality of opportunity for both students and academics. Indian higher education professionals, particularly technicians, are highly regarded and are considered amongst the best in the world, being in great demand internationally (Kaul, 2006). This illustrates a strength and quality in much of the Indian higher education system.

The professionalisation of academics in China is taking on increasing significance. Not always previously required, doctorates are now a general requirement for tutors at Chinese universities as China looks to the West as a benchmark of high quality provision. Increasingly, doctorates gained overseas are held in higher esteem by both universities and students and so are becoming an increasing requirement for academics. This creates an issue for the Chinese government, who having encouraged potential academics to undertake doctoral study overseas then have to attract them back to China to work or teach. The government is trying to entice those who study overseas by providing high-class facilities and good salaries. Those who are still not willing to return to their homeland are often invited to become visiting or associate professors at Chinese universities to ensure that Chinese higher education gains some benefit from them.

The notion of professionalism is an issue in the USA too, with institutions recognising that preparation as a researcher or scholar does not necessarily make one a good teacher. As in Britain, some institutions have undertaken a range of faculty development initiatives to help scholars become better teachers, with formal departments of Teaching and Learning providing support for faculty who want to become better in the classroom.

As well as ensuring high-quality teaching, many academics around the world are having to change how they teach in response to changes in the student body and the increasing perception that higher education is a product and therefore that teaching should take place as and when it most suits student needs, both discussed earlier in this chapter. Technology is playing an increasingly important role in this as Trevitt identifies:

Universities face an abundance of pressures to adapt and change at the outset of a new millennium. Changes in student participation rates and composition of student cohorts give rise to many new challenges in relation to the teaching function alone. Technology is frequently seen as one means of enabling changes, especially in respect of the teaching function.

Trevitt, 2005, pages 57–58

Having to incorporate greater use of technology in your teaching links back to the need for academics to have training and development in professional skills discussed in the earlier paragraph.

There is a link between the funding of higher education and the professionalisation of academics in a salary scale that is seen to reflect high professional standards and world class teaching abilities. There has been much tension inside and outside of universities in England and Wales in recent years as a national pay-spine for academics has been introduced. This has insured that the issue of academic salaries has remained at the top of the agenda for unions, vice-chancellors and the government. A single-pay spine has also been introduced in Scotland.

Practical Task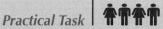

Academic salaries

Look at a selection of job advertisements for academic posts in England, Wales or Scotland. The best place to find these is in the weekly *Times Higher Education* magazine or on **www.jobs.ac.uk**. Sometimes university or higher education college posts are advertised in Tuesday's *Guardian* newspaper or the weekly *Times Educational Supplement*. Look at:

• the scale of the post: is it lecturer, senior lecturer or associate professor?
• the level of qualification required;
• the annual salary.

By looking at the first two bullet points you can compare the third in jobs that are like for like. Look at the different adverts collected by your group. Is there much difference in salaries between England, Wales and Scotland?

Find some job adverts for other professions (e.g. doctors, dentists, nurses, teachers, social workers, journalists or lawyers), by looking in newspapers or online. How do academic salaries compare to these? What might this suggest about the value placed on academic posts compared to other professions by society?

The *Times Higher Education* magazine often has adverts for academic posts in other countries. How do those that list the salary in pounds sterling compare with those in Britain you have found?

Traditionally, Indian academics have been financially *rewarded for longevity, rather than productivity, and for conformity rather than innovation* (Altbach and Jayaram, 2009, page 17). The current trend in India is to raise the salaries of academics in an attempt to keep the best and brightest staff in higher education rather than lose them to private-sector industries which generally pay enhanced salaries. The increased salaries require increased productivity in research and innovation in teaching and learning, mirroring developments in the UK and elsewhere.

China's economic reforms of the 1990s allowed universities there to engage in business activities. As a result of this many academics invested their time in money-making projects and students started to complain about reductions in the quality of teaching and contact time. Therefore, the Chinese Government has had to raise salaries of its academic staff in recent years to counteract this and encourage tutors to remain focused on their professional duties.

Remuneration for academics is an issue in the USA too, with faculty salary increases at US universities below inflation three times in four years. At the same time, salaries of senior administrators and sport coaches have increased significantly, making this particularly unpopular with teaching staff (Marcus, 2008) and creating a two-tier pay scale which the single pay-spine in Britain seeks to avoid.

Quality assurance and standards

The Dearing Report published in 1997 and referred to earlier, also recommended that the government's Quality Assurance Agency (QAA) assumed responsibility for ensuring all institutions in England, Scotland and Wales adopted a code of practice within a broad framework of qualifications which was universally understood and also allowed for easy credit transfer between institutions. Programme specifications have since been developed for every course which are published and clearly outline intended outcomes and points of exit.

As part of an increased focus on standards and accountability in English universities, institutions are required to adhere to more and more externally imposed processes and inspections. While this is meant to enhance the product, higher education, for the consumer, the student, this is not always the case. Crook *et al.* (2006) warn that a focus on procedures can mask actual problems in the activity itself. They give the example of student assessment which is a *well-ordered process* in most universities as being driven by audit requirements rather than students' educational needs, highlighting that increased accountability can have a negative impact on educational experience and satisfaction.

External examination of higher education colleges and universities is an increasing phenomenon in India and is tightly linked to government funding there. The University Grants Commissions is the key inspection agency and the primary awarder of government grants to institutions. You can see from the Indian system how funding and standards, or quality, are interlinked.

In China the inspecting body for higher education, and so the keeper of quality assurance, is the Ministry of Education. It undertakes annual inspections of each university, focusing on teaching and learning. A yearly inspection is criticised by the universities for being too frequent as they inevitably take the focus away from the students while academics prepare the bureaucratic necessities. As in India, it is the same government department that both inspects quality and then allocates funding, creating a direct link between the two.

In the US, external agencies, such as the National Curriculum Authority, periodically examine and accredit (or refuse to accredit) institutions as a whole or particular pre-professional programmes at those institutions, for example, teacher education, nursing or social work. The process of applying for and gaining accreditation is fraught with paperwork and is becoming an increasing burden for American education: the public demands evidence of accountability, but in order to demonstrate on paper that they are accountable, the educators spend less time actually being accountable in their classrooms and labs. This is typical of what is happening in Britain too.

With a government emphasis on academic standards and high-quality teaching and learning opportunities, national university league tables are regularly published in Britain and other countries. While some academics support these as raising the standard of teaching as universities strive to enhance their positions on the ladder, research has shown that they do have an effect on staff morale, and can be demoralising to those employed in institutions with a low rating (Attwood, 2008). The publication of league tables is another example of higher education being seen as a product, something easily measurable for consumers' information.

The purpose of higher education

This chapter has so far focused on government influence on universities through funding, expansion, professionalism and standards. The level of influence exerted in Britain is high as the government, through tax payers' money, is the primary funder of most universities and managed by the various higher education funding councils. With public funding come certain expectations and requirements which limit university freedom. However, while having to meet such demands as those identified above (in relation to widening participation, for example), many universities remain creative in their activities, driven by institutional missions and values to uphold freedom of academic debate by staff and students.

Reflective Task

What is the purpose of higher education?

Reference has already been made in this chapter to the purpose of higher education. Historically, in the USA there has been a focus on betterment, improving the individual's status and prospects in society, and thus improving society for everyone. It could be suggested that the US has been somewhat schizophrenic about higher education. It has been both a privilege for those who can afford and benefit from it, and a prerequisite to advancement in society. Coming to universal agreement on the purposes of higher education would be difficult at best as it depends on an individual's or country's political, philosophical and social perspectives.

- Based on government concerns discussed in this chapter, what do you think the British government sees as the purpose of higher education?
- How does the British government's view relate to governments in other countries, particularly India and China? In a group investigate different countries to see what the stated purpose of higher education is there. For example, is it for the good of individual students or for the benefit of society generally? Consider how the political system of that country might influence this.
- Given government control through funding, reflect on how, in your experience, universities try to be individual and unique places of learning. Compare your experiences across your group. You might want to look at mission statements of different universities, which affect the ethos of the individual institutions.

Some universities have traditionally chosen to focus on the pursuit and development of new knowledge. These institutions rely heavily on research funding from external sources alongside their government funds for teaching students. Research is a key activity for universities as it is one means by which they can increase their funding. Currently government-funded, leading-edge research contracts are awarded to a relatively small number of British universities; however, all universities in England are expected to develop a strong research base and this is assessed publicly every four to six years with research funding going to those institutions which can demonstrate their expertise. With this strategy, assessing each university's research ability and linking it to additional government funding, all universities are rushing to develop research. However, in other countries such as Germany and the Netherlands, top-quality or world-class research is concentrated in a few institutions allowing benefits from a concentration of human and non-human resources (DfES, 2003a). India is adopting this approach with the establishment of a National Institute of Technology which has top-class research centres at five universities across the country. China is developing ten world-class universities in which it will focus its research centres. The USA is adopting a similar strategy, concentrating world-class research in a minority of specialist institutions.

Most, if not all, universities in the world acknowledge that higher education is a process of personal development for students in that it provides them a space to consider their own place in the world and to think much more broadly than just about the academic discipline they are studying. Research by Burchell and Dyson (2005) recognises the importance of a place for reflection whatever is being studied. They suggest that *potential for learning is enhanced by setting up a place for reflection* (page 298). In some universities such an ethos is encouraged with an emphasis on students' holistic development. However, increasingly people view higher education as a product linked to a higher economic income and curriculum development has to match student demand in order for a university to recruit viable student numbers.

Student experience

As the student body diversifies, so the student experience might become increasingly varied. With the introduction of student fees and an increase in students from low-income families more and more students are having to work part-time to fund their time at university, not just in the UK but in many other countries, including those discussed here. Inevitably this takes some of the focus away from their studies and changes the way students view studying. Research by Prosser and Trigwell (1999) confirmed *that students enter learning and teaching contexts in higher education with varying perceptions of the context and their situation* (page 72). Those who see themselves as failing are less likely to respond to opportunities to develop their learning or to establish positive relationships with peers and tutors. Retention has become a major issue for some British universities as their government funding is based on student numbers at the end of the academic year.

There is an increase in mature students (those aged over 21) in Britain and Europe. Some of these have family commitments to manage alongside their studying. Consequently many are now driven by assessments, concerned with their measurable outcomes, namely their final degree classifications, particularly as massification of higher education has increased competition for graduate jobs. Mufti calls academics to recognise this and the increasing external demands made on students and to be aware that *higher education may not be the main focus of their lives at present, merely one part of it* (Mufti, 2006, page 131). The increase in students holding down part-time, or even in some cases full-time jobs, while studying is not specific to the UK but is a worldwide issue.

Higher education fees in India remain relatively low compared to the general cost of living and fees in other countries. While many middle or upper class students do not need to take on paid employment to fund their studies, there is an increase in students in paid work as the number of students from low socio-economic backgrounds is increasing. Similarly the numbers of mature students is increasing but at a slower level than in many other countries, including

Britain and China. These students experience conflicting demands on their time as they often juggle studying with paid employment and family commitments.

China has seen an increase in mature students too as previous regulations limiting opportunities for those aged 25 and over have been removed (Duan, 2003). The biggest concern for all students in China is whether or not they will be able to get a graduate-level job on completion of their degrees. While this is less of an issue for those studying in the top ten national universities, it is an increasing issue for others given the increasing number of student places against a decreasing graduate job market.

Students in the USA fall into three major categories:

- those who attend residential colleges immediately after their high school graduation;
- those who attend local colleges either full- or part-time, while still living at home or in another non-college setting; and
- those who spend some time after high school working or raising a family before returning to take college classes, either as full-time or part-time mature students.

Paid employment is an increasing necessity for American students, as for many others. As well as providing a financial means to exist while studying it can also help to provide both independence and identity. Mature students may be seeking independence as learners and an identity of their own, unrelated to their family commitment or employment category while younger learners may be seeking independence from their families for the first time. Of course independence and identity are not just of concern to American students but to many students regardless of their nationality, as entry into higher education often marks the shift from childhood to adulthood.

Increasing numbers of students around the world are having opportunities to study abroad. This is due to a rapid increase in international partnerships and regional co-operation within the global higher education sector. Some students may physically study abroad for the duration of a full degree or undertake smaller periods of study in another country where their university facilitates such flexibility. The Bologna Agreement, which sets out a common international framework of academic levels and awards, is making this much easier. Alternatively, increasing numbers of students are taking online courses, or parts of courses, based at institutions in other countries and so interacting virtually with overseas faculty.

Practical Task

Higher education in other countries

The Organisation for Economic Co-operation and Development (OECD) gathers a wide range of data from its 30 member countries. You can access the education data via the OECD website available at **www.oecd.org** or in a hard copy of a recent report, such as OECD (2007) *Education at a Glance 2007*. Paris: OECD.

Divide into small groups, preferably into pairs. Look at the OECD education data and select two of the member countries that you have a particular interest in and compare their statistics on higher education.

Analyse the data and look for similarities and differences.

- How do they compare on university graduation rates?
- How do they compare on employment rates and educational attainment, by gender?

- How do they compare on distribution of public and private expenditure on higher education?

Are these fair comparisons? Are the countries you compare starting from the same baseline? Does this matter? What other OECD data might you want to look at to judge this?

Chapter Summary

This chapter has discussed key issues facing universities and higher education colleges around the world.

- It has highlighted those which most affect Britain, in that they are at the top of the government agenda. They can be summarised as funding, expansion, professionalisation and quality assurance.
- While these four issues are central drivers for higher education institutions in England, Wales and Scotland, they are also of major significance to many other countries.
- Particular examples have been given illustrating how they affect universities in India, China and the USA but many of the trends discussed are global.
- Government influence over universities remains strong in most countries, with some governments exerting very tight control largely through funding policies.
- Against this the higher education marketplace is becoming increasingly competitive and institutions are having to develop clear, strong, saleable identities.
- This can create a dilemma for universities as they have to balance conformity to government requirements or targets with creativity and uniqueness to attract increasing numbers of students.

Of course, it is no surprise that all of the issues discussed in this chapter are inter-related. Higher education in the twenty-first century is increasingly about doing more with less, getting better value for taxpayers' and students' money, working to ensure that higher education is not only for the wealthy elites, and preserving academic freedom and quality.

Research focus

Comparative higher education

A seminal text on higher education, examining key issues in a number of different countries is:

- Tight, M (ed.) (2004) *The RoutledgeFalmer reader in higher education*. Abingdon: Routledge-Falmer.

Within this text you will find contemporary research from key international academics discussing issues such as funding of higher education through an international survey and graduate employment in selected countries. It enables you to consider a variety of research-based articles which explore the themes in this chapter. Which chapters you choose to read will depend on your interests but the following relates well to the funding issues discussed in this chapter and is recommended to you:

- Jongbloed, B and Vossensteyn, H (2004) Keeping up performances: an international survey of performance-based funding in higher education, in Tight 2004: 250–269.

As you read, pay particular attention to:

- what the authors consider to be the key issues in higher education funding;
- the extent that the countries referred to differ from each other and from those in this chapter;
- what research methods were used and whether or not the authors compared like for like in their survey.

Models of higher education

- Figueroa, FE (2008) European influences in Chilean and Mexican higher education. *European Education* 40, 1: 63–77.

This takes an interesting comparative education look at the influence of one country on another, in this case in the context of higher education. It presents three models of university government: the continental model, the British model and the American model. Make notes with particular reference to the Bologna process and how this is influencing universities in the countries under scrutiny.

Higher education in China

An excellent read on higher education in China is the following chapter:

- Levin, H and Xu, Z (2006) Issues in the expansion of higher education in the People's Republic of China, in Lauder, H, Brown, P, Dillabough, J and Halsey, AH (eds) *Education, Globalisation and Social Change*. Oxford: Oxford University Press.

It explores in considerable detail the issues involved in expanding the capacity of higher education in contemporary China to facilitate the participation of more students, including those from diverse backgrounds. In doing so it develops some of the points made here. While a few issues are specific to China itself, the majority of issues are global, faced by universities around the world in countries where expansion is a key driver. Think carefully about what implications the situation in China has for other countries you are interested in.

References

Altbach, PG and Jayaram, N (2009) India's effort to join 21st-century higher education. *International Higher Education Newsletter* 54: 154.

Attwood, R (2008) A measured relationship. *Times Higher Education* 10–16 April, 1, 840: 36–40.

Baker, M (2007) China's bid for world domination. *BBC World News*, 7 November 2007. Available at: **http://news.bbc.co.uk/1/hi/education/7098561.stm** (accessed 7 May 2009).

Barton, L (2003) The politics of education for all, in Nind, M, Rix, J, Sheehy, K and Simmons, K (eds) *Inclusive education: Diverse perspectives*. London: David Fulton, 57–64.

Beaumont, C (2007) Is full-time higher education a myth? *Pedagogical Research in Maximising Education* 2, 1: 15–25.

Burchell, H and Dyson, J (2005) Action research in higher education: Exploring ways of creating and holding the space for reflection. *Educational Action Research* 13, 2: 291–300.

Crook, C, Gross, H and Dymott, R (2006) Assessment relationships in higher education: The tension of process and practice. *British Educational Research Journal* 32, 1: 95–114.

Dearing, R (1997) *The Dearing report: National committee of inquiry into higher education*. London: The Stationery Office Limited.

DfES (2003a) *White paper: The future of higher education*. London: The Stationery Office Limited.

DfES (2006) *Widening participation in higher education*. London: The Stationery Office Limited.

Duan, X (2003) Chinese higher education enters a new era. *Academe Online* November-December. Available at: **www.aaup.org/AAUP/pubsres/academe/2003/ND/Feat/duan.htm** (accessed 7 May 2009).

Figueroa, FE (2008) European influences in Chilean and Mexican higher education. *European Education* 40, 1: 63–77.

Jongbloed, B and Vossensteyn, H (2004) Keeping up performances: An international survey of performance-based funding in higher education, in Tight 2004: 250–269.

Law, WW (2006) Education reform for national competitiveness in a global age: The experience and struggle of China, in Mazurek, K and Winzer, M (eds) *Schooling around the world*. Boston: Pearson, 68–103.

Kaul, S (2006) *Higher education in India: Seizing the opportunity (Working Paper No. 179)*. New Delhi: Indian Council for Research on International Economic Relations.

Levin, H and Xu, Z (2006) Issues in the expansion of higher education in the People's Republic of China, in Lauder, H, Brown, P, Dillabough, J and Halsey, AH (eds) *Education, globalisation and social change*. Oxford: Oxford University Press.

Marcus, J (2008) American faculty cry foul over pay. *Times Higher Education* 17–23 April, 1, 841: 15.

Mufti, E (2006) New students: Same old structures, in Kassem, D, Mufti, E and Robinson, J (eds) *Education studies, issues and critical perspectives*. Maidenhead: Open University Press, 122–132.

OECD (2007) *Education at a glance 2007*. Paris: OECD Publishing.

Prosser, M and Trigwell, K (1999) *Understanding learning and teaching: The experience in higher education*. Philadelphia, PA: Open University Press.

Riddell, S (2005) New Labour, social justice and disabled students in higher education. *British Educational Research Journal* 31, 5: 623–643.

Smith, B, Mayer, J and Fritschler, AL (2008) *Closed minds: Politics and ideologies in American universities*. New York: Brookings Institution Press.

Tight, M (ed.) (2004) *The RoutledgeFalmer reader in higher education*. Abingdon: Routledge-Falmer.

Trevitt, C (2005) Universities learning to learn? Inventing flexible (e) learning through first and second order action research. *Educational Action Research* 13, 1: 57–84.

Chapter 6

Teacher education in a changing context

David Cumberland, Wendy Bignold and Bart McGettrick

Learning outcomes

By the end of this chapter you should be able to:

- discuss the impact of historical and sociological developments in education on current teacher education requirements in England and elsewhere;
- understand the significance of teacher education for effective schooling;
- identify key reasons for government interest in teacher education and means by which governments influence teacher education;
- recognise and debate key issues and questions in teacher education at the start of the twenty-first century. For example, what is the role of the teacher today, and what should trainee teachers thus be prepared for?

Chapter outline

This chapter discusses teacher education for the compulsory school sector in Britain and Poland. It considers a number of different perspectives and significant changes over time to enable you to understand the current context in each of the two countries. It then explores key issues such as the curriculum for student teachers and the role of the teacher which students are trained to take on. Teacher education in Poland is interesting because it largely still relies on the disciplines of education set in a rapidly changing 'post-Communist' society. The pace of change of society is related to curriculum reform and there is a need to balance social change with curriculum planning.

The importance of skilled and effective teachers in the quality of schooling is increasingly recognised both nationally and internationally. Therefore, it follows that the quality of teacher education is of great significance to a country in the education of its future generations. The Australian government, for example, acknowledged this and undertook a review of national and international trends in teacher education:

With increased evidence that the quality of our teachers is the most important educational resource in our schools, greater attention is being given to factors that shape that quality. These undoubtedly include the capacity of teacher education providers to attract able students and to prepare them well to meet the demands of teaching.

Ingvarson *et al.*, 2006, page 1

Teacher education refers to both *initial teacher education and training*, courses for students who are preparing to become teachers, and *continuing professional development* (CPD), for existing teachers who wish to enhance their skills and knowledge. This chapter is largely concerned with initial teacher education.

Education in the UK has a varied and complex history. Changes in the education system have inevitably led to changes in teacher education and training because *teacher education, of course, plays a pivotal role in schooling* (Cole, 2006, page 207). There has been a shift from seeing teachers as delivery agents of a defined body of knowledge, to seeing them as facilitators and leaders in learning who are equipped to help pupils develop transferable personal learning and thinking skills underpinned by subject knowledge. This has inevitably led to the needs for a wider awareness of the role of teachers and the context within which they are working.

Historical *Perspective*

Schools before teacher education

Educational opportunities for pupils and teachers in England have varied over time but have largely been dependent upon income, status and location. The earliest schools were charities or privately funded and the quality of teachers, therefore, was hugely variable. In England in the early 1800s, for example, teachers were expected to impart knowledge to pupils rather than be skilled in the methods of teaching and understanding how pupils learn. Public schools would expect a high level of subject knowledge in their teachers, usually requiring the minimum of degree level experience, often from Oxford and Cambridge. Whereas, at the other end of the spectrum schooling, where it existed, might be little more than a small-scale, informal agreement for childminding, with a local 'dame' who would have had no formal education herself and be able to provide only the very basics in numbers and letters, if at all.

The growth of England as an industrial nation led to a greater need for schooling in order to ensure a skilled workforce. It became apparent by the latter part of the nineteenth century that the above system was simply not providing educated citizens in sufficient numbers. In 1870 the government realised that it needed to encourage a national system of education and passed the Elementary Education Act, known as the Forster Act. This allowed for towns and cities to provide schools for five- to twelve-year-olds, funded from local rates, with additional funding from central government dependent on inspection results. The use of public funds demanded a level of accountability of teachers. The school boards who ran these schools needed to ensure that their teacher employees could provide a far better quality of education than previously, whereby pupils would be able to read and write with fluency and expression and have a knowledge of basic mathematics, up to and including fractions.

Developing a profession

The increase in education provision, as in the number of pupil places, has had a significant impact on the recruitment and training of teachers and on successive governments' involvement in that process. Whilst early education acts provided for schooling no reference was made to the training of teachers or the methods of teaching, only the final outcomes in pupil assessment. The quality of teaching was inspected but there was no formal guidance on how to achieve quality. Teachers, therefore, tended to have a reasonable level of education but no specific teaching qualifications until the introduction of the Certificate in Education (Cert Ed.). It was not until 1963 and the Robbins Report that a degree route into teaching was finally established with the Bachelor of Education (B. Ed.). At this point other routes were also available in the form of diplomas and postgraduate certificates in education (PGCE) but these were very much in the minority and were taken primarily by those wishing to teach in the more academic grammar or independent schools. Since then there has been a shift to a minimum of graduate entry for the teaching profession. The Cert Ed. was abandoned in the 1980s and in March 2008 the Secretary of State for Education announced that teaching should be a masters level profession (Balls, 2008). Interestingly this decision was taken after looking at teacher education and levels of qualifications in other countries, in particular Australia, Hong Kong and Japan.

Practical Task

What should teacher education and training include?

Over the course of a week look at local and national newspapers for any stories on education. How are teachers portrayed in the media? Is it generally in a positive or negative light?

Thinking back to your own experiences as a pupil, and any recent experiences as a student or volunteer in school, what do you think are the key qualities and requirements of an effective teacher? Can these be taught?

Before reading further in this chapter, make a group list of things which you think should be included in teacher education or training courses. This might be, for example:

• an exploration of what learning is; health and safety procedures when taking children on a school trip.

One is philosophical, the other practical. Are both of equal importance in your view? Explain your answer to your group.

Keep this task at your side while you read this chapter. Are the areas for teacher education that you have identified seen as significant by government or teacher educators?

Sociological *Perspective*

Teacher education as a driver for social change

The development of education as a force in social change was made explicit at the beginning of 'The Great Debate' on school standards which was initiated in the Ruskin Speech by British Prime Minister James Callaghan in 1976. This speech heralded the importance of education as a significant political pressure point and a vital part of the contemporary social system.

Despite comments from previous governments that Britain was now a 'classless' society it is evident that, even at the start of the twenty-first century, there are still great divisions in the quality of education experienced and in the opportunities provided. Educational achievement was, and still is, strongly linked to social class, income, gender and ethnicity as this recent news report demonstrates:

A child's chances of achieving the benchmark of five good GCSEs including Maths and English, are heavily influenced by social background. Children brought up in low income households are much less likely to succeed than children of successful, financially secure parents.

McSmith, 2008, page 9

Of course, these issues of inequality did not just affect education but were well illustrated by it. They did, and do, however touch all aspects of family life:

. . . despite the progress that has been made if you are an ethnic minority Briton, you are still more likely to be stopped by the police, be excluded from school, suffer poorer health treatment and live in poor housing.

Johnson, 2007

The government has long recognised the power of education as a lever for social change and in the late 1990s schools were seen as partners in the agenda for social cohesion and inclusion. A citizenship education programme was established within the National Curriculum which required specifically trained teachers. Whilst a lot of money was spent on re-training those already in the profession a significant amount was also allocated to the training of new teachers in Citizenship. In the most recently published standards for qualified teacher status, reference is made to teachers' responsibilities for social cohesion and inclusion, ensuring its place in the school curriculum and so in the curriculum of student teachers. Interestingly, the role of teachers in the promotion of citizenship amongst children was recognised at a similar time with a centre for citizenship education set up in Warsaw, Poland, in the early 1990s (Tomiak, 2002).

As well as changes to the curriculum, it was recognised that changes had to be made in the drive to recruit potential teachers. If educational inequalities were to be addressed then pupils had to be taught by relevant role-models who they could aspire to become. This would require a significant increase in the numbers of minority ethnic students training to become teachers for all age-phases. and male students training, for example, to become early years and primary teachers. As a result of this universities and other providers of initial teacher education were set specific recruitment targets. This example and the citizenship curriculum illustrate how social policy can and does impact on teacher education.

Curriculum change

In the 1980s the prime minister Margaret Thatcher, concerned by liberal and free-thinking interpretation of education and education methodology, established for the first time in England a national curriculum. This was a weighty document which not only outlined expected skills and outcomes but also content. That is, it defined what was to be taught, with strong guidelines of when and how. Prior to this teachers had complete freedom to teach what they thought appropriate and relevant. A multitude of assessment targets were brought in and many teachers resorted to a tick-box approach with a concomitant loss of spontaneity and creativity. The testing regime which accompanied the National Curriculum became embedded in the practices of teachers. This led to a teacher education system characterised by the same rigidity. The Teacher Training Agency (TTA) was established and took its lead from what was happening in schools. This was a predictable model, but it implied a view of the teacher as an agent of the state whose task was to *deliver* the curriculum – a curriculum technician.

This centralist approach to education and teacher education in England government put pressure on other parts of the UK. In Wales there was a broadly similar national curriculum to that introduced in England, but with components special to Wales, Curriculum Cymreig. It was largely based on the same thinking but it did not have the same rigidity of testing associated with it.

In Northern Ireland there was also a tendency towards a more tightly controlled system. The political issues of the time, however, namely friction and fighting between Protestant and Catholic communities, allowed government to be pre-occupied with other matters, but there was a deep concern for issues of national unity. This resulted in the emergence of 'Integrated Schools' which were to avoid the sectarian divide between the Catholic and Protestant communities. These schools still struggled to find widespread acceptance across the communities. Developments in the school curriculum illustrated this concern over community cohesion with initiatives such as the programme for 'Education for Mutual Understanding'.

In Scotland, however, there was no appetite for a national curriculum. Instead the Scottish Consultative Council on the Curriculum, later to be known as 'Learning and Teaching Scotland', issued guidelines for curriculum and assessment for pupils aged five to fourteen. Despite pressure, this proved a sufficiently robust and acceptable framework for teachers and teacher educators to work from. For a variety of reasons, such as tradition, pride in the identity of the Scottish system, and wishing to avoid the perceived excessive governmental account-ability, the Scottish system remained fiercely independent. This stance became even stronger with the devolution to a Scottish Parliament in 1999.

Many in education saw this tightening of government control, illustrated through a set curriculum and prescribed pupil testing, as a loss of freedom and professionalism and a shift towards the teacher as 'technician'. This was true for teacher educators too who were required to train teachers to meet the new requirements. University faculties of education began to see their role threatened, particularly on postgraduate teacher training courses where a greater emphasis was being given to school-based training, for example with the introduction of *school-centred initial teacher training* programmes (SCITTs), which remain as alternatives to university-based courses today.

Changes in the modern social context

The abuse and murder of Victoria Climbié, an eight-year-old girl, at the hands of her guardians and carers in February 2000 led to an entire rethink of the wider children's services, including education. Victoria was known to a variety of agencies, including social services and child protection teams, but the lack of co-ordination between services led to ineffective and unco-ordinated action being taken. The government inquiry, headed by Lord Laming, made a number of recommendations that have significantly impacted on the way that all those who work with children and young people, including teachers, operate. The government's response was a policy document entitled *Every Child Matters: Change for children* (DfES, 2004). Five outcomes were identified for all children:

- be healthy;
- stay safe;
- enjoy and achieve;
- make a positive contribution;
- achieve economic well-being.

These outcomes have come to underpin all aspects of teacher education and ensure that there is a focus on:

- the link between children and young people's achievements and well-being;
- support for children and young people facing challenging circumstances;

- maximising opportunities for children and young people to reach their full potential;
- minimising risks.

Developing at the same time was the government's response to concerns about teachers' workload and quality of education and learning provided by schools. The *National agreement on raising standards and tackling workload* (DfES, 2003) attempted to reduce time spent on administrative tasks and cover for absent colleagues by teachers. It also aimed to provide defined time for planning preparation and assessment.

A third major influence on the context of teacher education was the prospectus *Extended schools: Access to opportunities and services for all* (DfES, 2005) which introduced extended schools and the notion of wrap-around care. These were new educational facilities that could be open from early morning breakfast clubs to evening leisure, social and educational classes. Within these centres would be housed a range of services, not just schools but health, youth justice, social services and so on.

The teacher's role in this changing context

This new context, integrating education with general well-being of children, requires teachers to be working as part of integrated teams of professionals focused on the needs of the child. Within these teams each would have their own area of expertise and specialism and ensure a holistic approach to children and young people's welfare and development. The teacher's role is crucial, although not necessarily a lead one. It is the teacher's responsibility to develop educational opportunities and lead learning for the child in collaboration with other educational professions, such as classroom assistants, learning mentors and not forgetting the role of parents, including fathers and carers. Where necessary teachers should be able to consult with, work alongside and within multi-disciplinary teams, including social and health workers, in meeting the child's individual needs. Such diversity of practice has major implications for the training of teachers, where teachers, particularly in secondary schools might previously have focused almost entirely on their subject specialism and viewed themselves as teachers of maths or English, for example. They now have much wider responsibilities and must be trained to contribute to the wider children's workforce.

The training of teachers in a changing context

As part of a drive to regulate and improve the quality of the teaching workforce, the government gradually increased its control over teacher training. In 1998 it identified a set of professional standards that all teachers should meet in order to receive registered qualified teacher status (QTS) with the Department for Education and Science (DfES). This was a requirement for all those who would teach in state-maintained schools in England and Wales. The first set of standards might be regarded largely as a set of 'can do' statements outlining the expectations of the teacher's role in terms of curriculum knowledge and skills. Subsequent revision of these standards have seen a paradigm shift away from knowledge of content to standards that are underpinned by the ECM outcome above, with a focus on holistic development and team working, not just in schools but in a range of educational settings.

Critical Thinking Task

Interpreting the Standards

The current Professional Standards for Qualified Teacher Status in England can be found at the TDA website: **www.tda.gov.uk/partners/ittstandards/guidance_08/qts.aspx**. They are divided into three categories:

* attributes; knowledge and understanding; skills.

Read the standards Q3 to Q6 under the headings 'Frameworks' and 'Communicating and working with others'. Think critically about how these particular standards apply to the current context for which student teachers are being trained, specifically in relation to the Every Child Matters agenda discussed above.

Read the standards Q14 and Q15 under the heading 'Subjects and curriculum'. What do they suggest to you about government control of the curriculum? How might they be interpreted differently for an early years student teacher, a primary student teacher and a secondary student teacher?

Read the standards Q18 to Q21 under the headings 'Achievement and diversity' and; 'Health and well-being'. How do these standards relate to social justice and inter-agency working for which student teachers are now being educated? What evidence might a student teacher produce to demonstrate they had met these standards?

This shift away from specific knowledge has also been seen within the curriculum itself. The most recent revision to the curriculum in England has seen far greater freedom being given back to the teacher in curriculum choice and delivery style, with a greater emphasis on cross-curricular working and the development of transferable learning and thinking skills. This has led to the re-emergence of the teacher as a creative and reflective professional with greater autonomy, yet within a more widely defined workforce. One could argue, however, that these changes have not seen greater freedom given to teacher educators, whose role is now more closely defined and inspected than even before. OFSTED, the Office for Standards in Education, regularly inspects teacher training programmes which are, as Pickard suggests, *rigorously policed* (2006, page 14). As a result, teacher education is increasingly influenced, or even controlled, by the government.

Political *Perspective*

Government control of teacher education

Until the middle of the twentieth century, government showed little interest in teacher education. This was not the case for churches and in the early part of the twentieth century, local groups of 'teacher educators' started to emerge. After World War Two, education became potentially much more significant and so attracted more government interest. Universities were mainly interested in postgraduate activities and to a limited extent in aspects of research and scholarly thought.

For ten years, prior to 1994, teacher education in England was overseen by the Council for Accreditation of Teacher Education (CATE). For the first time, the number of days of school-based training was defined as 100 days for undergraduates and 75 days for postgraduate students and established the beginnings of a partnership between schools and higher education in teacher education provision. In 1994 the Teacher Training Agency (TTA), now called the Training and Development Agency for Schools (TDA) was established to replace CATE. This marked a significant shift in government thinking and control. It *was more powerful than CATE and more directly under ministerial control* (Alexander, 2001, page 142). The professional development of teachers was no longer 'education' but 'training'. The Agency also had responsibility for the recruitment, quality assurance (assessment and curriculum), accreditation and funding of teacher training, all heavily influenced and regulated by the government (McNamara *et al.*, 2008). It could also be argued that as the Agency's remit only extended to England, this point saw the beginning of marked differences in teacher training and education between England, Scotland and Wales. The TDA now has responsibility for the continuing professional development of teachers which was previously largely the remit of local authorities, as well as other educators and school staff.

Government influence has extended with the creation and formation of the General Teaching Council (GTC) for England and separately for Wales in 2000. Scotland has had its own GTC for over forty years. The Teaching and Higher Education Act (1998) which established the GTC for England and for Wales called for the councils to *contribute to improving standards of teaching and the quality of learning and to maintain and improve standards of professional conduct among teachers, in the interests of the public* (HMSO, 1998, page 2). The various GTCs maintain registers of all qualified teachers in their constituent countries of England, Scotland and Wales, and are involved in the professional regulation of teachers. As such, these regulatory bodies are significant in ensuring the quality of teacher education and also in developing programmes for the continuing development of teachers.

This chapter has, so far, explored the changing context of education in England and the related context of initial teacher education. It is impossible to consider one without the other. Key themes have been the curriculum, the role of the teacher and the influence of the government. Let us now consider these with regard to recent developments in teacher education in Poland.

Teacher education in Poland

In Poland there has been considerable government reflection on teacher education in recent years, accompanied by ongoing changes in educational legislation. In particular, there has been a movement towards greater precision in teacher education, taking its guidelines from changes in the wider education system. Teacher education there is preparing teachers for the education system and is also offering a critique of that system. Teacher education is a preparation for engaging with pupils in schools and other educational settings, but is also reflective of that process. Teacher education can never be distant or removed from the education system but neither can it become so immersed in it that it loses perspective. To form and educate leaders in an education system it is necessary to have some external reference points. This is not effective if the horizons of teacher development are those of a single education system.

As in England initial teacher education in Poland has received much interest in recent times, triggered too by government concern over the quality of teaching:

Initial teacher education has been the subject of attention in Poland for many years in respect of both its organisation and content of studies . . . much greater stress was being put on the transmission of theoretical knowledge than upon its application in practice.

Tomiak, 2002, pages 101–102

In Poland, there are two main options for those who wish to become teachers. One route is to undertake a three-year Bachelor degree in teacher studies at a university. Alternatively, students can study for three years at a teacher education college and if successful gain a teaching qualification too, but not a BA degree. This route is available for those wishing to teaching in primary or secondary schools. In reality the majority of those who wish to teach at secondary level take a two-year Master's programme after their three years of undergraduate study. This focuses almost entirely on their specialist subject as they are already deemed to have been trained in educational philosophy and practice. This expectation of secondary teachers to be trained to masters level with primary teachers entering the profession at pre-Master's level can be seen to create a two-tier system with different status accorded to teachers of different levels. The emphasis on subject specialism for secondary trainee teachers and a more general or broader programme of study for primary teachers is the same as in the UK and many other countries and is driven largely by the curriculum the trainee is expected to teach.

It was only in 1989 that communist rule ended in Poland. Prior to this there was a very rigid national curriculum in keeping with communist philosophy. Indeed there was only one publishing house allowed to publish textbooks for schools until 1989 and teachers were trained to be technicians. As Poland has sought to lose its Soviet traditions and modernise itself, it has looked towards the West, and now Europe of which it is a part, for guidance. There have been major educational reforms in the country in 1983, 1984 and 1990 which promoted discussion and debate *on the kind of school that would meet social expectations, be 'student-friendly' and allow a comprehensive development of personality'* (Pirog and Tracz, 2003, page 165). A wide range of stakeholders, including teachers, psychologists and educators, were involved in subsequent further reforms and the Ministry of Education introduced a new national curriculum in 1999. Similar in structure to that taught in English schools, it sets out a basic curriculum with a range of syllabuses from which teachers can choose, selecting those which they feel are most suitable or of interest to their pupils and their context. The 1999 reform of the Polish education system not only introduced a new curriculum but also the concept of curriculum planning and suggested methods of teaching, as well as a new systems of exams and teacher evaluation of pupils' learning. This impacts on teacher education as trainees must be prepared to teach the National Curriculum and must be able to select those elements of it over which they have choice. To do this they need to be more than simply technicians of the curriculum and must be able to recognise the individual and collective needs of their pupils. Interestingly, according to OECD statistics, primary school teachers in Poland have, on average, 21 pupils in each class (compared to 26 pupils in a UK class). Smaller class sizes may enable Polish teachers to know their pupils more intimately than their UK counterparts (OECD, 2007). Of course it will take some time for these changes to work through the school system as new teachers are trained and educated in new ways of teaching with a more child-centred focus. Meanwhile some teachers still deliver the curriculum in rather formal ways, with an emphasis on didactics. That would even be true of areas such as citizenship.

The education system in Poland is not simply driven by a concern for pupil development. As in most, if not all, other countries the education system is also strongly influenced by the need to educate the workforce of the future. This is particularly so for countries which are seeking to modernise quickly and develop their economy. This practical need also impacts on teachers and teacher educators and has influenced a more practical approach to the new National Curriculum:

Recent changes however also put emphasis on the need for economical development, focusing on the participation in the European market economy. This leads to a more pragmatic approach.

Snoek *et al.*, 2003, page 139

The developments in the Polish National Curriculum discussed run parallel to changing views on the role of the teacher. Increasingly teachers are not delivering the curriculum, but planning learning opportunities which enable pupils to develop to their full potential. This focus on individual pupils' development can be seen in the earlier quote from Pirog and Tracz (2003). Indeed there is increasing emphasis on learner-centred pedagogy rather than the traditional teacher-centred pedagogy. Thinking back to recent developments in England with Every Child Matters and the need to prepare trainee teachers to work with other professions and agencies to meet the whole needs of the child, something similar, but less defined is happening in Poland. The less strict social climate which has developed in recent years has created increased pressures on children and young people. Teachers are expected to be aware of these in order to support pupils' welfare and development as well as educational achievement:

All this may serve as an indication of the additional responsibilities of teachers and teacher educators alike. Acting 'in loco parentis', they have a duty to protect the children and young people they teach from the new dangers that can no longer be ignored.

Tomiak, 2002, page 105

As in the UK then, the role that teachers, and so teacher educators, have to play in the development of society in post-communist Poland, to create a genuinely free and open society, is increasingly recognised. Teacher education is seen as a significant force in promoting social cohesion in the country (Snoek *et al.*, 2003).

Reflective Task

Similarities in teacher education programmes in England and Poland

Below is an extract from a UNESCO World Education Forum report on Poland which can be accessed at **www.unesco.org/education/wef/countryreports/poland/rapport_3.html**. It describes developments in teacher education in 2000. Read the extract and carefully consider each statement.

The programmes of teacher studies will reflect the following new aspects:
- *The teacher will be susceptible to change teaching methods and prepare pupils for unexpected situations, instead of preserving traditional, old habits.*
- *The teacher will play the role of a guide assisting pupils to understand the world and take an active part in the process of changes, instead of transmitting narrow knowledge of separate subjects.*
- *The teacher will be prepared to perform his/her tasks both in the classroom and in the local environment.*
- *Integrated blocks of teaching contents, overall structures and processes will replace teaching strictly subject-oriented elements of knowledge.*
- *Training will be provided to teachers in the area of multimedia information technologies and communication systems (television, video, internet – for the purpose of distance learning and virtual school).*

Reflect back on what you have already read about teacher education in England. What similarities can you see between Poland and England? Look at bullet point 3 in this box, for example. It refers to teaching *in the classroom and in the local environment*. In England, partly as a result of Every Child Matters, trainee teachers have to be ready to teach in a broad range of settings. This could be referred to as *the local environment*.

Do you think teacher education is primarily to 'deliver the curriculum' or to open the minds of teachers to see education as a liberating condition for a better society?

Government influence on teacher education in Poland

There are a number of ways in which national governments can influence, or manage, teacher education. Some of these have been discussed in relation to England. These include managing the curriculum, funding teacher training institutions, accrediting professional programmes and inspecting provision. European governments, like many others, want to be able to measure the standards of teacher education in their various countries in order to manage quality and ensure standards of teaching in schools are raised or enhanced. Of 30 European countries examined by the European Commission's Directorate-General for Education and Culture, all except Luxembourg *have a regulated system for evaluating initial teacher education* (Eurydice, 2006, page 9). Poland was part of this study and has two different systems. Teacher training colleges are inspected by the Ministry of Education and, as such, are directly evaluated by the government. University departments offering teacher education, on the other hand, are inspected by the Polish State Accreditation Committee, acting on behalf of the government. This is much like the TDA does in England. This implies a greater level of autonomy to universities over teacher training colleges. Teacher training colleges are governed by school legislation (Eurydice, 2006), as opposed to higher education regulations which may be one reason for the difference in autonomy accorded. However, Eurydice (2002) earlier recorded that all Polish institutions providing initial teacher education for lower secondary education, had the same level of autonomy, which it reported to be limited. This confirms a high degree of government influence in teacher education there.

Comparative teacher education

The quote below is from the Head of Improvement in Initial Teacher Training at the TDA.

Trainee teachers need a range of learning opportunities to enable them to be well prepared to contribute as NQTs (newly qualified teachers) to the workforce. These learning opportunities need to be based on a clear understanding of the changing context within which teachers are working and the teacher's role and responsibility within that context. They need to develop an understanding of the school and children's workforce that the teacher may contribute to and how to contribute effectively to ensure children and young people's achievement and well being.

Rowe, 2006, page 3

While Rowe was referring to trainee teachers in the UK she could equally be referring to trainee teachers in any country, as the example of Poland has demonstrated. Most, if not all, countries would probably now agree that it is a teacher's role to strive to ensure their pupils' achievement and well-being. They may, however, have different strategies for doing this, underpinned by culturally specific philosophies. This will lead to both similarities and differences in teacher education globally.

In an increasingly global world of education the mobility of teachers across Europe and beyond has meant that there is a move to adopt frameworks for teacher development that facilitate the engagement of teachers in different countries. This professional mobility, access to the internet, and ease of travel all lead to greater internationalisation. With this greater concern for international capability comes the interesting opposite tendency to wish to emphasise local cultural identity. Education systems are not culturally neutral. They are the product of the cultural ebb and flow of modern life. Teacher educators recognise and work with the opportunities and paradoxes which these bring.

Chapter Summary

This chapter has discussed initial teacher education and its changing context in the UK and Poland, with both countries having to rethink how teachers are trained.

* There is greater specialisation as we understand more and more about learning and about child development. This increase in knowledge and understanding is crucial in a university environment. For many this is a huge strength, although there is also a need to have this increase in understanding applied in schools and other educational settings.
* At the same time there is recognition of the need to look at integrated approaches to working with other professions and working in an inter-disciplinary way.
* In professional practices the emergence of 'Children's Services' and other kinds of developments has made it necessary for the teacher to interact at a professional level with many other professional groups. This has an impact on the kind of professional education that is necessary for those who bring an educational perspective to integrated practice.
* This acknowledges that it is not possible to consider the child as a developing person without considering the wider social and family circumstances in which the child is growing. Education is not simply about 'delivering the curriculum' (a meaningless phrase!) but about facilitating the relationships for the child to promote the total flourishing of all gifts, abilities and talents. This lies at the heart of teacher education.

Research focus

Task 1

A key publication for education students, the *World yearbook of education*, focused specifically on teacher education in its 2002 edition. Given its focus on teacher education, it is still of significance to today's student of comparative education.

* Thomas, E (ed.) (2002) *World yearbook of education 2002: Teacher education, dilemmas and prospects*. London: Kogan Page.

It examines this key aspect of national education systems from a variety of perspectives and different countries, including England and Poland. It also examines South Korea, Argentina, Spain, Brazil and Israel, amongst others.

It has a particularly interesting section entitled 'Cultural perspectives and the education of teachers'. Culture is, as you will be aware by now, hugely significant in comparative education.

You are advised, therefore, to read and consider this section carefully to further your research on teacher education.

Task 2

A significant article of its time, and still referred to today is:

- Gilroy, DP (1992) The political rape of initial teacher education in England and Wales. *Journal of Education for Teaching* 18, 1: 5–22.

Gilroy is very critical of the government's approach to teacher education and training. He sees this approach as being very controlling of the process and also as abusive to teacher educators. Read the article and try to identify what he bases his views on. Do you think he is justified in taking such a strong anti-government stance? Make notes on any areas that link to your reading of this chapter as a way of extending your understanding of the context and issues of teacher education.

Task 3

What do you think you have learnt from this chapter? What has it added to your understanding of teacher education? Is this learning relevant to your work?

References

Alexander, R (2001) *Culture and pedagogy: International comparisons in primary education*. Oxford: Blackwell.

Balls, E (2008) *Party conference speech*, Labour Party Spring Conference, Birmingham.

Cole, M (2006) New Labour, globalisation and social justice, in Kassem, D, Mufti, E and Robinson, J (eds.) (2006) *Education studies: Issues and critical perspectives*. Maidenhead: Open University Press, 201–210.

DfES (2003) *The national agreement on raising standards and tackling workload*. London: DfES.

DfES (2004) *Every Child Matters: Change for children*. London: DfES.

DfES (2005) *Extended schools: Access to opportunities and services for all*. London: DfES.

Eurydice (2002) *The teaching profession in Europe. Report 1: Initial training and transition to working life*. Brussels: European Commission, Directorate-General for Education and Culture.

Eurydice (2006) *Quality assurance in teacher education in Europe*. Brussels: European Commission, Directorate-General for Education and Culture.

Gilroy, DP (1992) The political rape of initial teacher education in England and Wales. *Journal of Education for Teaching* 18, 1: 5–22.

HMSO (1998) *Teaching and higher education act*. London: HMSO.

Ingvarson, L, Elliott, A, Kleinhemz, E and Mckenzie, P (2006) *Teacher education accreditation: A review of national and international trends and practice*. Sydney: Australian Institute for Teaching and School Leadership Ltd.

Johnson, N (2007) CRE launches final legacy document: 'A lot done, a lot to do: Our vision for an integrated Britain'. Available at: **http://83.137.212.42/sitearchive/cre/default.aspx. locid-0hgnew0zk.Lang-EN.html** (accessed 7 May 2009).

McNamara, O, Brundrett, M and Webb, R (2008) Primary teachers: Initial education, continuing professional development and school leadership development. *Primary Review Research Survey* 6, 3

McSmith, A (2008) The big question: Has the divide between Britain's social classes really narrowed? *The Independent* 4 November. Available at: **www.independent.co.uk/news/uk/home-news/the-big-question-has-the-divide-between-britains-social-classes-really-narrowed-989 660.html** (accessed 7 May 2009)

OECD (2007) *Education at a glance.* Paris: OECD.

Pickard, A (2006) What is worth knowing in education studies, in Sharp, J, Ward, S and Hankin, L (eds) *Education Studies: An issues-based approach.* Exeter: Learning Matters, 12–19.

Pirog, D and Tracz, M (2003) The status of geography in the Polish education system. *International Research in Geographical and Environmental Education* 12: 164–170.

Rowe, L (2006) 'Every Child Matters: The role of the teacher in the changing context'. Teacher Development Agency discussion paper, TDA/UCET Conference, 4 July 2006, page 3.

Snoek, M, Nogueira, F, Halstead, V, Hilton, G, Mikl, J, Rehn, J, Sousa, JM, Stomp, L and Viebahn, P (2003) Reflections on trends in teacher education in Europe using the scenario perspective. *European Journal of Teacher Education* 26, 1: 137–142.

Thomas, E (ed.) (2002) *World yearbook of education 2002: Teacher education, dilemmas and prospects.* London: Kogan Page.

Tomiak, J (2002) Teacher education in Poland: Reform and reassessment, in Thomas 2002.

Chapter 7

Education and social care: friends or foes?

Sue Kay-Flowers

Learning outcomes

By the end of this chapter you should be able to:

- recognise the importance of the United Nations Convention on the Rights of the Child (UNCRC) on children's right to education and explore the concept of social care within the UNCRC;
- understand what is meant by the terms 'ethnocentrism' and 'cultural relativism';
- discuss the social construction of childhood in different countries;
- recognise that social policies relating to children and young people are located in time and place, drawing on the examples of England and Romania;
- investigate the relationship between societal understandings of childhood and the development of social policy.

Chapter outline

This chapter considers global issues in relation to social welfare, the impact of political and economic systems on the development of social care and moves by some countries towards integration of social care and education. It is not seeking to compare different systems as such but rather to develop insight through looking at countries with significantly different recent histories, England and Romania.

It is increasingly recognised that education does not take place in a vacuum with teachers working in isolation from other professionals concerned with the well-being of children and young people. The movement to provide joined-up services is growing in momentum worldwide. The United Nations Convention on the Rights of the Child (UNCRC) offers a useful framework for considering education and social care issues in an international context, setting out as it does an internationally agreed set of rights for children. However, in looking at international comparisons there is a need to guard against ethnocentrism and cultural relativist standpoints, concepts that will be explored further within this chapter.

The sociology of childhood has shown how understandings of 'childhood' are located in time and place and therefore how childhood is 'socially constructed' within different societies. The concept of social construction of childhood will be examined and its influence on the development of social policies relating to children and young people discussed in order to explore the relationship between education and social care in some systems and their integration in some countries. The contrasting experiences of an affluent, industrialised West European country, England, and a country in transition following a period of communist rule, Romania, will be explored.

The United Nations Convention on the Rights of the Child (UNCRC)

Every country in the world, with the exceptions of the USA and Somalia, is a signatory to the UNCRC and so it is useful to refer to this international convention when looking at the position of children in any country. The convention contains 54 articles (points) in which children's rights are recognised and obligations placed on states (governments) to recognise these rights in practice. According to Alderson the UNCRC *concentrates on adults' responsibilities to protect and provide for children and young people* (2003, page 11). She categorises the articles into three groups, often referred to as the '3 Ps'.

- provision;
- protection;
- participation.

More recently, however, the provision articles have been subdivided into survival and developmental. The provision of services relating to children's right to education and social care will be the main focus of this chapter although it is important to recognise many children's rights are intertwined across the three different categories of provision, protection and participation.

The definition of a 'child' under the convention is anyone under the age of 18. Article 2 sets out that each country shall ensure that the rights expounded in the convention are available to all children within their borders without discrimination of any kind. Progress on implementing these rights is monitored by the Committee on the Rights of the Child, which is composed of experts from different countries. Non-fulfilment of these rights is seen as a matter of discrimination.

In their most recent report submitted to the UN inspectors, the four Children's Commissioners for England, Scotland, Wales and Northern Ireland identified the following infringements of the UNCRC which they say deny:

hope and opportunity to many of Britain's 14 million children and adolescents; a punitive juvenile justice system; public attitudes that demonise teenagers; lack of protection against physical punishment in the home and one of the highest levels of child poverty in Europe.

Carvel, 2008, page 3

A report submitted for Romania (UNICEF, 2006) expressed concern in relation to discrimination of Roma children, children with HIV/AIDS and children with disabilities and recommended that Romania effectively implements existing legal measures to address these issues. Roma people comprise a tribal ethnic group originally from South Asia but now widely spread out across Europe with a sizeable population in Romania.

Practical Task

Children's rights to education and social care within the UNCRC

The full list of children's rights in the UNCRC can be found on the United Nations International Children's Emergency Fund (UNICEF) website at **www.unicef.org.uk/youth voice/pdfs/uncrc.pdf**. Take time to read these rights carefully to ensure you understand them fully as they are significant to this chapter and to your study of education generally with its focus on children and young people. The main articles within the UNCRC relevant to children's right to social care are Articles 3, 8, 9, 12 and 19. Take time to read these articles carefully to ensure you understand their meaning, making detailed notes. When the article refers to *parties,* it means the countries that are signatories to the Convention.

Articles 28 and 29 in the convention refer particularly to children's rights on education so make detailed notes on these. Consider Article 28 carefully and answer the following questions:

- How are primary, secondary and higher education organised in your country?
- Is the right to education available to all children in your country on an equal basis or are some children less represented at different stages of the education system?
- Which groups of children are most likely to experience difficulties in exercising their right to education? Why do you think this is so?
- How would you describe your country, as an industrialised western country, as a country in transition or as a developing country? How and why might this impact on children's rights to education?

Ethnocentrism and cultural relativism

In looking at the experience of 'childhood' and the development of services in other countries there is a need to guard against adopting an 'ethnocentric' approach. An ethnocentric approach is when a person looks at, and evaluates, the experience of other countries against their own norms and values. Ethnocentrism can be defined as *the habit or tendency to judge or interpret other cultures according to the criteria of one's own culture,* and is probably a universal tendency (Seymour-Smith, 1986, page 97). This definition is still used by academics and practitioners today (Sanders, 2004). A danger in adopting an ethnocentric approach is *the tendency to view one's own culture as best and to judge the behaviour and beliefs of culturally different people by one's own standards* (Kottak, 1994, page 48). Most children raised in England have been required to attend school betweenthe ages of five and sixteen, with penalties imposed on their parents if they do not ensure attendance. Their education, as well as exercise books, textbooks, scientific equipment and often the cost of travel to and from the school will have been paid for by the state. Such children will inevitably adopt certain norms and values as a result of this experience and will use them to make judgements about education in England. However, this same set of norms and values would not be helpful in understanding and assessing education in, for example, a rural Romanian village.

In exploring comparative perspectives it is better to adopt a 'cultural relativist' approach whereby understanding of society is gained by seeking an understanding of that community within its own context and in its own terms.

Greenwood and Stini give a definition of cultural relativism that is still useful today:

Cultural relativism involves understanding another culture in its own terms sympathetically enough so that the culture appears to be a coherent and meaningful design for living.

Greenwood and Stini, 1977, page 182

Returning to the example of Romania, although it is a requirement that children attend primary school, many primary-school-aged children in rural areas do not attend on a full-time basis and it is important to have an understanding of the reasons why. To help with the task of adopting a culturally relativist viewpoint it is necessary to know something about families in such communities. Many families, for example:

- are economically very poor;
- work on the land as subsistence farmers;
- often require their older children to help them in the fields or to look after younger siblings while they work so the family has enough food to eat;
- cannot afford schooling because, whilst it is 'free', pupils are required to buy their own exercise books, pens, pencils and so on.

This information may lead to a change of previously held views and adoption of a more empathetic, cultural relativist view, recognising the local context.

There are dilemmas in adopting a cultural relativist standpoint, as Sanders (2004) points out:

It would be an oversimplification to say that ethnocentrism is an unmitigated evil, and that cultural relativism is an unequivocal good . . . . The dangers of an ethnocentric perspective are relatively clear. It is a manifestation of the exercise of power imbalances between different cultures and societies . . . with cultural relativism one lacks a foundation from which to censure female circumcision, the internment of Jewish children (and adults) in concentration camps, the historical practice of foot-binding in China . . . . At its most extreme, cultural relativism would imply the acceptance of such practices on the basis of being only comprehensible within the culture in which they are/were practised, and not susceptible to external judgement.

Sanders, 1999, page 27

While many of the practices identified above would gain little sympathy amongst the general population in most societies today, some of these issues, such as female circumcision, are ongoing, and the question is then raised of how members of one culture can tell those of another what to do.

International agreements such as the UNCRC seek to overcome some of these difficulties by setting down an internationally agreed set of values to which all societies subscribe. In doing so it is recognised that not all countries have the same starting point in terms of resources (such as people, skills, infrastructure and finance) to practise these values and therefore may need the support of others in achieving them. Most significantly though, they offer a universal view of the rights of children, thereby setting an important agenda around which debates about children's situations can take place and against which individual countries can be held accountable for their actions to the United Nations Committee on the Rights of the Child.

Social construction of childhood in different countries

To develop further understandings of education in a comparative sense it is necessary to have an appreciation of the social construction of childhood. In other words to understand how societies and cultures construct and inform our notions of what it means to be a child – and therefore how childhood is experienced within a particular society and how this differs across time and across place (between countries and cultures). The question, 'What is a child?', for example, may lead to some discussion about the different ages at which individuals cease to be children and become adults. The United Nations' definition of a child as someone under the age of 18 would probably meet with broad agreement. However, if the question 'What is childhood?' were to be asked, this would lead to much wider debate with considerable differences likely across countries or cultures.

Reflective Task

Childhood in different countries

Work through the following task with a group of fellow students. Keep a record of your discussions to help you understand the rest of this chapter.

Read the following quote and pick out what you think are the key phrases:

In modern society, childhood is usually thought of as a natural set of experiences suitable to individuals at this early stage of human development. Childhood is protected and respected, free from (adult) worries and responsibilities, a time of learning and play, a period of happiness and relative freedom.

Lavalette and Cunningham, 2002, page 9

- Do you think this reflects contemporary experiences of childhood in England or other parts of the UK?
- How might particular concepts of class, gender, welfare systems, employment and education impact on what it means to be a child?

In order to make sense of the concept of the social construction of childhood look at the experience of a typical Roma child living in a very poor area of rural Romania and then answer the questions.

Maria is 12 years old and the third child in a family of eight children. She lives with her parents and siblings in their house which consists of one room in which the family live, eat and sleep. The room is in a very poor state of repair with a hole in the roof covered in plastic. In winter the temperatures can reach as low as -20°C. Her parents and older brothers have occasional work in the fields but employment is erratic and money very limited. Like most children in the area she has just one meal a day and is often hungry through lack of food. Her youngest sister has just had her first birthday and so her mother leaves her with Maria while she goes out each day to look for work. Maria went to the village primary school until recently. She enjoyed learning and her attendance was quite good but now that she has to look after her sister she cannot attend school and so she spends all her time in the Roma village.

- What are the issues preventing Maria from exercising her right to education?
- How do the experiences of family life and school for children in the UK compare to the experience of the Roma child? Reflect on your own childhood.
- What are the main differences and similarities in children's experience of childhood, regardless of their country?
- Ask a friend or relative from a different generation to yourself to tell you about his or her own childhood. How does this differ from your experience?

The rationale for studying the experience of childhood in other countries is often to throw light on one's own society by drawing attention to, or problematising, issues. In other words it strips away notions about childhood within one's own country which may be taken for granted. It makes for interesting reading and raises significant questions about how children's lives are organised, their independence and notions of 'children's space'. In this way it offers challenges to assumptions about childhood within each society and provides a sociological perspective on childhood and education.

Sociological *Perspective*

From her work comparing children's experience of growing up in England with the experience of growing up in Finland, Mayall has drawn general conclusions relating to the way children's lives are *constructed* (Mayall, 2002) which can be used to consider the construction of childhood in different countries. In particular she identifies the following contexts as being the most significant in the social construction of childhood within society:

- the state, the family and children;
- attitudes towards protecting children from 'traffic danger' and 'stranger danger';
- gender issues in the division of labour;
- education.

Mayall also points to underlying class differences in England which remain a strong influence on children.

Extensive work in this area has been undertaken by Qvortrup (1993). He identified three key elements within the social construction of childhood:

- childhood is a permanent category within society but the experience of childhood changes *across time and space*;
- childhood is not isolated from society but is affected by societal changes and events (for example think of how major world events such as the destruction of the World Trade Center in New York in 2001 affect children);
- children are themselves co-constructors of childhood and society; in other words they are active participants in society and influence and determine the experience of being a child within a particular society.

These elements are also recognised by James and Prout (1997), who go on to suggest that, as such, children's social relationships and cultures are worthy of study in their own right, independent of adults. As childhood is a variable of social analysis, it also cannot be divorced entirely from other factors such as class, gender and ethnicity all of which serve to ensure that children within a particular society experience 'childhood' differently.

The development of social care policies in England

During World War Two, England and Romania experienced very different social, economic and political climates and these contrasting experiences highlight how social policies and legislation are directly influenced by time and place.

England had enjoyed a long period of stability and security, allowing a strong democracy to develop which had been able to build up national resources to fund a welfare state. The welfare state was established after World War Two and a key focus of social policy in the UK as a whole is on social welfare or care provision. 'Welfare' is considered to comprise two parts. The first is 'well-being', the security, happiness and comfort that individuals seek or have a right to. The second aspect is 'help given to people in need', the provision of welfare services to particular social groups whose members lack well-being. Policy makers have the responsibility to decide who is in need, how to prioritise that need and address it appropriately. Responses may be through the provision of services and/or benefits, targeted at a particular group or available to all (Walsh et al., 2000).

The experiences of World War Two, particularly the evacuation of children living in the cities, meant the general population of England had become aware of the very large social divisions within its society. Those in rural areas learned of the poor living conditions of inner-city children first-hand and there was a desire to improve living conditions for all – hence the notion of providing for those 'in need' from 'the cradle to the grave'. The pillars of the welfare state were established in the mid-1940s and include:

- free compulsory education for all children;
- free health services for all at the point of delivery, provided by the National Health Service;
- a social security system to provide a financial safety net for those 'in need' such as the unemployed and the sick.

In addition, universal child benefit was introduced to provide a minimum level of financial support to all parents raising children. These services were to be funded through the payment of National Insurance contributions paid by all those of working age and in employment. The aim was to provide a level of welfare provision from which all families could benefit according to their particular needs. Education and social welfare, health and social security were all seen as key parts to the welfare state, thus linking them together, although with no integration of services at that time.

The original concept of the welfare state, as it was conceived in the 1940s, still underpins UK society – education and social welfare are available free to all citizens. That said, since its inception there has been considerable debate about who is in need and what the priorities of the welfare state should be. It has not proved easy to achieve 'equality' for all children and families in practice, despite strong ideals. Class background, for example, remains a significant determinant in life chances and quality of services available. The opportunity remains for those families with personal financial resources to pay for private schooling and health care, thus bypassing waiting lists and ensuring high quality.

The development of social care policies in Romania

Romania, in contrast to England, has had a turbulent and complex history, at times linked to neighbouring countries – Greece, Turkey, Saxon Germany, the Soviet Union and Hungary. It has experienced waves of migrating peoples, each leaving their mark on the local culture and language, and creating ongoing change. Modern Romania was formed after World War One when Romania more than doubled its territory and its population grew from 7 million in 1912 to 18 million in 1930 (Boia, 2001). World War Two resulted in Romania being forced to give parts of the country to Hungary, Bulgaria and the Soviet Union, but in 1944 Romania changed allegiance, allying itself to Russia, thereby salvaging its independence and shortening the war. At the end of World War Two the monarchy was abolished and communism was installed in a predominantly rural country. Of the 22 million people living in Romania today, approximately 50 per cent live in rural areas, significantly higher than in England where the equivalent figure is less than 20 per cent of the population.

The communist era saw a particularly repressive and authoritarian rule which was to heavily influence the formation of values over 40 years (UNICEF, 2006). The most significant communist leader was Nicolae Ceauşescu who came to power in 1965 and ruled until he was overthrown in the revolution of 1989 and executed. The fundamental principle under-pinning the communist social welfare system was that the state was the provider of education and social care services. The difference between this and the democratic state provision in the UK, was the development of state control imposed through the social welfare system in Romania.

Ceauşescu believed that for Romania to be 'great' there was a need for more citizens, and so a pro-natalist policy was introduced where families were expected to have at least five children with the communist party controlling family life (UNICEF, 2006). As family size grew without the financial resources to match, many parents were unable to provide suitable living conditions or food for their children. At the same time the state promoted values and norms which viewed giving up a child to public care as acceptable. The institutionalisation of children became normal and was often seen as in the best interest of the child. Health staff promoted institutionalisation as something positive, particularly if the child had any health problems. As children with health issues or disabilities or those whose parents were unable to provide for their children's day-to-day needs as a result of poverty were put into institutions, social welfare assistance for the family became unnecessary as social problems were *officially non-existent* (UNICEF, 2006). Welfare support was provided through state-run institutions rather than individual families, as in England.

In 1991 there were as many as 700 institutions for children in Romania. This includes 112 institutions for children under the age of three (UNICEF, 2006). It was estimated that over 100,000 Romanian children lived in institutions at that time. Severe economic deprivation limited resources and the subsequent development of services. Social workers were trained at a much lower level than previously and so were not well equipped to meet the needs of children:

traditionally, institutions were designed to shelter large numbers of children, were staffed with people insufficiently qualified for this type of work, and were entirely unsuited to provide children with the care they needed. The involvement of parents in the lives of the children was reduced or non-existent.

UNICEF, 2006, page 42

During the communist era:

the synchronising of the Romanian educational system with that of European countries, which was achieved between the two World Wars, was continuously degraded.
  Coposescu, 2002, page 16 cited by Crawford, Walker and Granescu 2006, page 488

Consequently the quality of education regressed and it was seen as unrelated to social care.

Integration of social care and education in England

The UK has signed up to the UNCRC and has given some aspects of it legal status by includ-ing some of its articles in the Children Acts of 1989 and 2004. The most significant policy development of recent times in England has been the introduction of the 'Every Child Matters' (ECM) policy in 2003. This followed a government inquiry into the tragic death of an eight-year-old girl, Victoria Climbié, who died following extensive abuse and neglect.

The report highlighted significant errors in communication between those agencies with a responsibility to protect children – social services, health services and the police. The failure of inter-agency co-operation was seen as a significant need in the social policy reform that was to follow.

Contemporary English understandings about children and young people were reflected in the process of policy development and the policy itself. The government needed to address and respond to the failures within the child protection system but it also sought to ensure children and young people's participation in making the policy. In line with Article 12 (*the right to express an opinion and to have that opinion taken into account on any matter affecting them*), children were asked to identify the key issues they believed were important in ensuring a good and safe childhood. This was done through face to face consultation with various groups of young people including those who historically had been marginalised such as 'looked after children' (those in care) as well as through the internet to allow comment and feedback on policy ideas. The consultation process also involved the views of practitioners working with children and young people, including social workers, youth leaders and teachers.

This process enabled the government to identify five key outcomes that were seen as essential to the promotion of children's well-being:

- be healthy;
- stay safe;
- enjoy and achieve;
- make a positive contribution;
- achieve economic well-being.

The policy set out the ways in which these outcomes could be achieved by identifying aims, support for parents, carers and families and targets as well as how its success would be measured (more detailed information can be found on the Every Child Matters website at **www.ecm.gov.uk**).

A number of fundamental ideas about current understandings of childhood were set centre-stage within this influential policy. Adopting a 'holistic view' of children in order to understand their development and progress more clearly was seen as essential to the outcomes being achieved. For example, previously teachers tended to view children mainly as learners while social workers' assessments focused on their social needs. However 'Every Child Matters' requires different agencies, including education, social care and health, and voluntary agencies (charities) to work together much more closely. In some cases this required legislation (The Children Act, 2004), in others further policy development (The Common Assessment Framework). In all cases it involved breaking down barriers between different professions in order to adopt a more integrated approach to working with children.

There was strong emphasis on the inclusion of all children, especially those with particular social, educational or medical needs, within mainstream educational systems and society in general. This concept was seen as beneficial not only for the individual child's development, but for all children and for wider society in general. Social inclusion was seen as an essential strategy in recognising diversity and building a more inclusive society. This emphasis was driven, in part, by the renewed commitment to social justice by the government. Policy across the UK, at the start of the twenty-first century, is to integrate social care and education.

Integration of social care and education in Romania

After the Revolution of 1989, Romania faced very great challenges in relation to the situation of its children. Ceauşescu's policies had left a devastating, painful and long-lasting legacy which Romania's new government needed to address with urgency. In 1990 Romania signed the UNCRC and adopted it as part of Romanian law. An immediate issue facing the country was the significant number of children living in institutions. Western journalists described the 'orphanages' they saw and the conditions within them. Widespread consternation and condemnation from Europe and the USA followed and yet the wider context was often not understood. This illustrates an ethnocentric approach taken by western media rather than a considered, cultural relativist approach. In many cases the term 'orphan' was a misnomer anyway. Many of the institutionalised children did have living relatives, but state policies had encouraged parents to leave their children in the care of the state in the belief they would be fed and have a better life.

There were insufficient numbers of trained staff to work in these institutions in the early 1990s and Romania had little chance of remedying this situation in the immediate short term. International assistance was provided with efforts focused on improving the situation of children in care and took the form of food, clothing, building programmes and developing new child welfare programmes. Trained social care workers and educators from outside Romania worked alongside each other as volunteers in the institutions, sharing knowledge and skills and developing good practice in order to professionalise the Romanian child protection system. Social work was reinstated as a profession in universities once more, leading to the development of social policy and social work practice (Roth-Szamoskozi *et al.*, 2008).

In 1997 a period of legal reform, modernisation and professionalisation started with the passing of two major pieces of child welfare legislation which addressed child protection and set out the responsibilities of public bodies. This led to the development of:

- support services that prioritised family care;
- 'family models' in residential child care centres so children of different ages could stay in the same home;
- a network of professional, paid foster parents called 'maternal assistants';
- child protection services with responsibility for the assessment and decision-making in alleged cases of child maltreatment.

In 2004, the Romanian government passed a Children's Rights law which promotes children's rights in all areas of life. This significant piece of legislation defined the responsibilities of professionals and promoted *collaboration* between private and public services protecting children, a key development recognising the important relationship between social care and education. Interestingly this was the same year that the UK government passed the Children Act promoting integration between professions, one step further than collaboration.

These policy and legislative reforms demonstrate how society's attitudes towards children have changed dramatically within the last 20 years in Romania, and to a lesser extent in the UK. Today Romania is developing a well-defined policy and practice taking into account the UNCRC which is incorporated into Romanian law. By contrast despite some articles being incorporated into the Children Acts of 1989 and 2004, in the UK the UNCRC remains only a policy, because the convention has not been enshrined in domestic law. However, the most recent UN Committee's Report (2008) recommends that the UK should look at ways of giving the articles legal status, possibly through a Bill of Rights. In Romania, as in the UK, the family is valued as a key social unit.

Whilst there are examples of collaboration between education and social care in Romania it is not without its difficulties. Roth-Szamoskozi *et al.* (2008) suggest that:

teachers are not prepared to address the problems of poor and neglected children; they have little supervised practice and practically no training or theoretical basis for working with children with special needs. There are no social workers in school system except from those working in some pilot projects . . . and a few child psychologists.

Roth-Szamoskozi *et al.*, 2008, page 81

Changes in policies over recent years have resulted in more highly qualified personnel being employed in children's welfare services. Despite this, there is still a desperate need for *child-centred educational services, especially in rural areas, which impedes on the school progress of a large number of children* (Roth-Szamoskozi et al., 2008, page 81).

Social policy and social change

Social policies, education and welfare need to be considered within a country's particular socio-economic, political and historic situation. This is a point readily accepted by the UN Committee on the Rights of the Child which recognises that in realising children's rights in practice account needs to be taken of each country's particular situation. There is a complex relationship between policy and legislative changes and society's attitudes. Sometimes policy reflects changing attitudes within society, but often it is the driving force which leads to a change in attitudes. Such changes can be far reaching and inevitably it takes time for a society to make the necessary social and psychological adjustments. Figure 7.1 attempts to summarise the ongoing cyclical process of how the development of policy can impact upon the outlook and behaviour of that society which in turn leads to a change in ideology, values and beliefs.

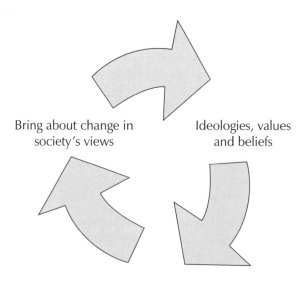

Bring about change in society's views

Ideologies, values and beliefs

Inform development of social policy

Figure 7.1 Cycle of social policy and attitude change

Critical Thinking Task

Policy views of the child

This task asks you to apply your knowledge and understanding of the development of social care policy in Romania and England, focusing in particular on the developing collaboration or integration of social care and education.

Think critically about how a child is viewed within the social policies for each country, past and present, justifying your answers. You might want to consider these questions to help you:

• Was/Is the child valued? What evidence do you have of this?
• Was/Is the child seen to have rights? What supports your answer?
• Were/Are the views of the child valued? If so, how is this demonstrated?
• Was/Is the role of the parents in child development and well-being recognised? What makes you think this?

Remaining challenges to integration in England

England has moved towards integration of children's services under the ECM policy, which adopts an holistic view of the child and requires interagency co-operation across education and social care services but also includes health services and the voluntary sector. There are many examples of excellent practice, for example in Children's Centres, Connexions Service and Extended Schools, but challenges remain in ensuring effective interagency working becomes the norm across all sectors – and that children with special educational needs or a disability are included in all areas of their lives.

While policy in England, and the rest of the UK, has seen a significant integration of children with disabilities over the last 20 years, some argue that individual needs are no longer taken into account as specialised facilities are closed down in favour of integrated provision. Despite the aims of Every Child Matters parents can often experience difficulty in accessing appropriate services to support their child who has a disability or who has special educational needs.

The two different approaches to children with special needs or disabilities in Romania and England illustrate the complexity of the issues surrounding the bringing together of education and social care. Despite striving to achieve interagency co-operation, England and the rest of the UK still faces significant challenges in this area. Indeed in November 2008 another young child died of abuse due to a lack of effective multi-agency working by those across child-protection agencies, suggesting the integration of services remains an ongoing challenge in practice.

Remaining challenges to integration in Romania

Romania remains a country in 'transition' and, as Roth-Szamoskozi *et al.* (2008) point out, there have been difficulties in achieving the desired changes in practice. This is predominantly due to the increased level of poverty that continues to affect children in Romania. In 1990 it was estimated that 7 per cent of the total population of Romania (22 million) lived in poverty, compared to 36 per cent by 2000 (World Bank figures). This significant increase affected the rural population disproportionately, 48 per cent of whom were seen to live in poverty. There has been a similar increase in extreme poverty over the same period from 9 per cent to 14 per cent with Roma communities being particularly affected by poverty. The recent global economic downturn is likely to have exacerbated the situation even further.

The new legislative measures introduced from the early 1990s were expected to be implemented within many of the old structures, with little priority given to the creation of new services (Roth-Szamoskozi et al., 2008). This remains a challenge for Romania and consequently the system is suffering from significant underfunding. There are inequalities in service provision across areas with some social services offices and some institutions unable to recruit sufficient staff. There are particular challenges in planning services for isolated rural communities with little infrastructure including transport links. It should be noted, of course, that Romania is not alone in grappling with some of these issues – certain parts of England experience similar issues in relation to recruitment and retention of appropriately trained staff. As a result, English service providers often have to employ trained staff from outside the UK including, ironically, Romania to fill vacancies. Rural communities in the England too sometimes face a reduced service compared to urban areas, often compounded by limited public transport.

There is no doubt that over the last 20 years Romania has faced great challenges in its social welfare provision for children and it has made considerable progress particularly in introducing legislative changes. It has incorporated the UNCRC into Romanian law and outlawed physical chastisement of children – two developments that England has yet to achieve, and there are moves towards greater collaboration in child protection. However, challenges remain in recruiting appropriately trained staff to implement these changes.

Specific issues remain in Romania, particularly in relation to children with significant disabilities, many of whom are still in residential homes and are therefore excluded from mainstream society and therefore cannot benefit from any collaboration between social care and education. Such children in residential institutions also have a complex set of needs relating to possible reintegration with birth families, the need for additional support and in some cases foster placements. It is recognised that Roma children are likely to be over-represented in this particular group because they are less likely to experience a foster or adoptive placement.

Chapter Summary

This chapter has identified some of the significant influences affecting the development of social care policy in relation to children and young people using the examples of England and Romania.

- The United Nations Convention on the Rights of the Child identifies a set of rights for those under the age of 18 which governments are expected to adhere to.
- When examining social policy and education in other countries we should guard against an ethnocentric approach and seek a cultural relativist view instead.
- 'Childhood' is a permanent category in society but the experience of childhood changes over time and space, being socially constructed.
- Policy makers' decision-making and priorities are influenced by their understandings of childhood. Therefore, policy making is located within the wider historic, political, social and economic context of the particular country being studied.
- In some countries, including England and Romania, there is a move towards the integration of services for children, including social care and education.
- The effective integration of children's services requires much commitment from government, policy makers, practitioners and society.

Research focus

Task 1

An interesting book to support this chapter is:

- Riddell, S and Tett, L (2001) *Education, social justice and inter-agency working: Joined-up or fractured policy?* London: Routledge.

It is also available as an e-book, published in 2002 by Taylor & Francis.

It presents a collection of academic papers all with a focus on interagency working and integrated services. The papers explore a number of themes, including social care, special educational needs, collaborative practice, special health needs and housing policy as it relates to education. As well as looking at England papers draw on different countries, such as America, Scotland, Japan, France and Australia.

Read the first chapter carefully, by way of an introduction, and make notes about why, in the editors' views, integrated policy is so high on government agendas today. Other key questions for you to consider while reading it are whether interagency working can achieve social change or not, and what the necessary conditions are for successful partnership working amongst different professionals and practitioners. Different chapters in the book will help you answer these questions in more detail so you are recommended to read those which relate to your particular interests, for example, early childhood education and care or children with disabilities.

Task 2

A fascinating book on childhood in England is:

- Madge, N (2006) *Children these days*. Bristol: Policy Press.

Madge gathered the views of 2,000 children and young people, as well as over 500 adults, to find what they thought about childhood in England at the start of the twenty-first century. Although this is not a comparative study it is fascinating as she gives voice to children and young people so you can read about their experiences as they interpret them rather than how policy makers interpret them. Madge acknowledges at the start that childhood is a social construct and several chapters explore this in more detail. As well as discussing key themes such as the meaning of childhood and children's rights and participation in society it is interesting in that she shares with the reader details of the research project itself, through which she gathered the views of the children.

You are particularly advised to read Chapter 10, 'Findings and Messages'. In this Madge articulates the messages that the children want us as adults and wider society to hear. Read this and make detailed notes then consider how integrated services, particularly education and social care, might address some of the things the children raise.

Task 3

In September 2006, the Children's Society of the UK commissioned 'The Good Childhood Inquiry'. This was the UK's first independent national inquiry into childhood. Its aims were to renew society's understanding of modern childhood and to inform, improve and inspire all our relationships with children. The report is interesting, timely and current:

- Layard, R and Dunn, J (2009) *A good childhood: Searching for values in a competitive age.* London: Penguin Books.

This book collates the evidence used to inform the report, the recommendations and summaries of the themes discussed in the report, as well as the response of the Children's Society. Read the report and make notes on the values it sees as significant to childhood.

References

Alderson, P (2003) *Institutional rites and rights*. London: Institute of Education.

Boia, L (2001) *Romania*. London: Reaktion Books.

Carvel, J (2008) Dossier prepared for UN details grim plight of many young people in Britain. The *Guardian* 9 June. Available at: **www.guardian.co.uk/society/2008/jun/09/children.youngpeople** (accessed 8 May 2009).

Crawford, K, Walker, J and Granescu, M (2006) Perspectives on social care practice in Romania: Supporting the development of professional learning and practice. *British Social Work* 36: 485–498.

Greenwood, DJ and Stini, WA (1977) *Nature, climate and human history*. New York: Harper and Row.

James, A and Prout, A (eds) (1997) *Constructing and reconstructing childhood: Contemporary issues in the sociological study of childhood,* 2nd edn. London: Falmer.

Kottak, CP (1994) *Anthropology: The exploration of human diversity*, 6th edn. New York: McGraw Hill.

Lavalette, M and Cunningham, S (2002) The sociology of childhood, in Goldson, B, Lavalette, M and McKechnie, J (eds) *Children, welfare and the state*. London: Sage.

Layard, R and Dunn, J (2009) *A good childhood: Searching for values in a competitive age*. London: Penguin Books.

Madge, N (2006) *Children these days*. Bristol: Policy Press.

Mayall, B (2002) *Towards a sociology for childhood: Thinking from children's lives*. Buckingham: Open University Press.

Qvortrup, J (ed.) (1993) *Childhood as a social phenomenon: Lessons from an international project*. Eurosocial Report 47. Vienna: European Centre.

Riddell, S and Tett, L (2001) *Education, Social justice and inter-agency working: Joined-up or fractured policy?* London: Routledge.

Roth-Szamoskozi, M, Popescu, L and Rat, C (2008) Changes in Romanian child welfare policies along the transition years, in Ilut, P (ed) *Dimensions of Domestic Space in Romania [Stari si fenomene ale spatiului domestic in Romania]*. Cluj-Napoca, Romania: Presa Universitara Clujeana.

Sanders, R (1999) *The management of child protection services: Context and change*. Aldershot: Arena.

Sanders, R (2004) Childhood in different cultures, in Maynard, T and Thomas, N (eds) *An introduction to Early Childhood Studies*. London: Sage.

Seymour-Smith, C (1986) *Macmillan dictionary of anthropology*. London: Macmillan.

UNICEF (2006) *Children on the brink: A focused situation analysis of vulnerable, excluded and discriminated Children in Romania*. Bucharest: Vanemonde.

Walsh, M, Stephens, P and Moore, S (2000) *Social policy and welfare*. Cheltenham: Stanley Thornes.

Chapter 8

Education for citizenship: different dimensions

Phil Bamber

Learning outcomes

By the end of this chapter you should be able to:

- define citizenship, global citizenship and citizenship education;
- recognise some of the historical, philosophical, political, social and economic influences on approaches to citizenship and citizenship education;
- outline case studies from England, the USA and India, identifying their different approaches to citizenship education, including formal schooling, volunteering and global citizenship;
- develop an understanding of the range of sites of citizenship education and associated pedagogies;
- critically analyse different frameworks for citizenship education by drawing on the case studies and your understanding of different concepts of citizenship.

Chapter outline

This chapter discusses citizenship and the theory underpinning citizenship education. The importance of education for active citizenship will be highlighted and it will be argued that a focus solely on citizenship of the nation state is no longer sufficient. It presents evolving approaches to this area, drawing on examples of practice from around the world. The specific examples are from England, America and India as they provide three different strategies for citizenship education. The chapter concludes by considering approaches to education for global citizenship: providing further insight into different responses to unprecedented global changes.

There are two dimensions to any definition of citizenship. Firstly, that citizenship is a status which is accompanied by a set of responsibilities and, secondly, that it is an entitlement to certain rights. Understanding the relationship between rights and responsibilities is therefore central to understanding citizenship in different contexts but for some this is insufficient. Osler and Starky (2005) argue that citizenship is also experienced as a feeling of belonging and therefore argue citizenship has three essential and complementary aspects: a status, a feeling and a practice. The importance of citizenship to the development of nation states is self evident and cannot be underestimated.

If the concept and institution of citizenship were suddenly erased from all human consciousness and behaviour, morality and justice would be acutely impaired.

Heater, 1990, page 314

The need for citizenship education is apparent if we accept citizenship incorporates these different dimensions. Although an individual has the status of citizen as a birthright, they must learn about the rights and responsibilities this status entails. A feeling of belonging is not automatic and must be nurtured. This implies that citizenship education is pivotal to the concept of citizenship itself. Of course, any programme of citizenship education is open to manipulation by the nation state to foster attitudes that help meet wider goals. This chapter will outline varying forms of citizenship education in different contexts and consider the rationale underpinning these initiatives.

Political *Perspective*

Political perspectives and political interests

Theoretical understandings of citizenship draw on theories of political science including liberalism, communitarianism and civic republicanism (Jochum *et al.*, 2005). A focus on the legal status of citizenship, such as in the United States of America, results in civics education that prioritises learning about national history and state institutions. The development of volunteering or service-learning opportunities in America reflects moves away from this liberal tradition towards a communitarian/civic republican understanding. Concerns about levels of community cohesion and engagement in the political process have encouraged countries such as England and the Netherlands towards an understanding of citizenship as a lever for social cohesion or civic engagement. In some, notably Asian, countries, a yearning to nurture identification with the nation state and a concern for its future has led to education that promotes a sense of national identity or patriotism.

Frameworks for citizenship and citizenship education

Globalisation has challenged nation states to reconsider their citizens' roles and responsibilities. The emergence of a truly global economy, the revolution in information and communications technology, the reality of climate change and worldwide migration, the end of the cold war and start of a global 'war on terror' have all served to blur boundaries between nations. What it means to be a citizen of a country has been placed under renewed scrutiny. National governments aspire for their young people to assume roles within the wider world yet expect that they also understand local and national developments. Meanwhile, without the existence of an internationally elected body, the 'global citizen' continues to have no formal status. These challenges have created opportunities for us to develop our understanding of the different dimensions of education for citizenship.

The concept of citizenship is complex and contested and therefore there are multiple dimensions of what is argued to be education for citizenship. Approaches to education for citizenship in any one country are informed by the way citizenship is framed in that particular context. This is influenced by a range of historical, philosophical, social, political, cultural and economic factors. In China, for example, education for citizenship is used to buttress the ideology of the communist party and the socialist system, promoting a set of distinct values and beliefs in keeping with communist ideology. In South Africa, a post-apartheid democratic society has emerged with leaders from both the black majority and ruling elite unable to draw on their own experience of or a tradition of democratic governance. In England, black and

Asian immigrants along with, more recently, so-called 'economic migrants' from eastern Europe have generated concern for the cohesion of communities which has resulted in the establishment of a written test for those who wish to attain British citizenship.

Different approaches to citizenship education can be placed on a continuum, from minimal to maximal (Osler and Starkey, 2005):

- Education *about* citizenship that provides students with knowledge of national political institutions and systems is indicative of a minimalist approach that could take place exclusively in the classroom.
- Education *for* citizenship reflects a maximal approach that aims to ensure students are ready to take on the role of adult citizens and associated responsibilities. This requires the development of relevant skills, values and attitudes to be an effective citizen, as opposed to simply the acquisition of knowledge and understanding.

An approach with maximum commitment demands that students participate actively in their own learning: it draws on theories of experiential learning. In schools, colleges or universities, the institutional culture may promote student voice through a student council. In the wider community, students may volunteer or carry out investigations for community groups.

This minimal/maximal continuum mirrors a parallel discussion that distinguishes 'citizenship' from 'active citizenship'. Active elements of citizenship involve engagement and participation in conventional political activities, voluntary community activities, or activities that seek to change political and social direction. Passive elements involve a sense of national identity, patriotism and loyalty. A thematic study of 14 countries, including Hungary, Canada and Singapore, in the INCA network (International Review of Curriculum and Assessment Frameworks) investigated policy and practice in an attempt to define 'active citizenship' across a range of contexts. It concludes that although any definition of 'active citizenship' remains problematic, the promotion of active citizenship *is linked to a more participatory form of citizenship which involves the development of citizenship education as an active process in a range of contexts in and beyond schools* (Kerr and Nelson, 2006, page iv). While education *about* citizenship requires little action on behalf of the students, effective education *for* citizenship is manifested in 'active citizenship'.

Citizenship education: a comparative study

The largest comparative study to date, the International Association for the Evaluation of Educational Achievement Civic Education Study (known as the IEA CIVED study), researched provision of citizenship, or civic, education across 28 countries. The study investigated how schools promote civic knowledge, attitudes and involvement and involved nationally representative samples of nearly 90,000 14-year-olds. Young people were assessed on:

- their knowledge of civic content (including state institutions, civil institutions and principles of equity and freedom);
- their skills in interpreting civic information (including their interpretations of announcements made through the media);
- their concepts of the role of citizens and the extent to which they intended to become involved in citizenship activity (such as voting, volunteering or involvement in community organisations).

The study accepted the contested and complex nature of citizenship and aimed to assess various cognitive, conceptual and attitudinal strands of education for citizenship. While the study assumes that the national political, social and cultural context informs the provision of citizenship education in different countries and also the formation of learners' perceptions of their role as citizens, the key findings (IEA, 2007) concluded that across these countries:

- Education for citizenship has a low status in many countries. Although teachers of citizenship or related areas value its importance to develop critical thinking, in practice most teaching of citizenship is didactic and content-based.
- Young people across countries have a positive sense of national identity (demonstrated through trust to the country as a political community, to government institutions, or to both).
- The main source of news for young people is the television.
- Although young people recognised the importance of voting, four out of five (80 per cent) showed no interest in other forms of political engagement, such as being a member of a political party or writing to newspapers to voice concerns about particular issues. Young people instead recognise activities, unrelated to electoral politics or political parties, as a way to demonstrate good citizenship, such as participation in community organisations, collecting money for social causes and participation in non-violent protest march.
- Young people prefer to belong to organisations in which they can work with peers and see the results of their efforts. The potential for youth organisations to positively influence the civic preparation for young people has been insufficiently exploited.
- Schools that model democratic practice (including an open climate for classroom discussion and the use of a student-led school council) are most effective in promoting civic knowledge and engagement. However, about a quarter of students (25 per cent) said they are rarely if ever encouraged to voice their own opinions.

Of course, the difficulties in constructing a meaningful, reliable and valid international survey across diverse political systems and cultural contexts should not be underestimated. It is of interest that the study considered only developed or middle-income democratic countries. Interestingly the study found that a diverse picture of civic knowledge and attitudes towards democratic participation does not conceal any underlying pattern dependent on whether a country is a newly-democratic (e.g. Poland, Latvia or India) or a long-established democracy (e.g. England, Greece or the USA).

Critical Thinking Task

Citizenship case studies

Having considered the theoretical underpinning of education for citizenship, this chapter will now look at a comparative study on citizenship education and then present three case studies. It does not seek to compare these; indeed the difficulties of doing so have already been raised. Instead as you are reading the case studies you are encouraged to think critically about what are the key similarities and differences in:

- understanding of citizenship;
- approaches to teaching citizenship;
- significance placed on learning through personal experience.

Education for citizenship in schools: England

(Case Study 1)

The 1988 Education Reform Act introduced the duty of maintained schools in England to provide a curriculum framed in academic terms as core (e.g. English, mathematics and science) and foundation subjects (e.g. history, geography and technology). Although this was seen to marginalise the teaching of the more social elements of education, the act also required this curriculum to promote the spiritual, moral, cultural, mental and physical development of pupils and of society in an aim to prepare pupils for the opportunities, responsibilities and experiences of adult life. Consequently, citizenship, along with health education, multicultural education, careers and economic understanding amongst others began to feature as cross-curricular themes through which schools were able to meet this aim.

There were well-publicised concerns regarding political apathy and anti-social behaviour in the 1990s. As a result of this on 19 November 1997, following proposals in the education White Paper, *Excellence in Schools*, the Secretary of State for Education and Employment pledged *to strengthen education for citizenship and the teaching of democracy in schools*, and appointed Professor Bernard Crick as Chair of an advisory group on citizenship education. The final report of the advisory group (QCA, 1998) recommended that the teaching of citizenship and democracy should be a statutory requirement and was followed by a government order to adopt these proposals alongside the implementation of the findings of a review of the national curriculum in general. The aims of the Crick Report, as it has become known, were indeed ambitious:

We aim for no less than a change in the political culture of this country: for people to think of themselves as active citizens, willing, able and equipped to have influence in public life.

QCA, 1998, para 1.4

The Crick Report proposed that three strands make up effective education for citizenship:

- *social and moral responsibility* – children learning, from the beginning, self-confidence and socially and morally responsible behaviour, both in and beyond the classroom, towards those in authority and towards each other;
- *community involvement* – children learning how to become helpfully involved in the life and concerns of their neighbourhood and communities, including learning through community involvement and service;
- *political literacy* – children learn about the institutions, issues, problems and practices of our democracy and how citizens can make themselves effective in public life, locally, regionally, and nationally, through skills as well as knowledge.

The influential report has however been criticised by scholars and commentators. It fails to view political activities beyond traditional forms, such as voting, at a time when youngsters are seen to be engaged in a multiplicity of social movements and when a failure to vote is often a political statement in itself. Although the report does outline in detail the key concepts, values and dispositions, skills and aptitudes, as well as knowledge and understanding, that are essential learning outcomes to be attained by the end of compulsory schooling, surprisingly it does not include amongst these definitions of concepts such as citizenship, society, nation-state, equality, solidarity and anti-racism. However, a more serious accusation has been raised, that the report reflects, rather than challenges, institutional racism in British Society through the use of *patronising language and stereotypes in its depiction of groups* (Osler, 2008, page 13), outdated understandings of multicultural education and a tendency to link minorities and diversity with conflict or problems.

Although a non-statutory framework for citizenship and PSHE at Key Stages 1 and 2 was introduced in 2000, citizenship finally established itself as a subject in its own right in 2002 when citizenship education became a statutory part of the national curriculum at Key Stages 3 and 4 (for pupils aged 11–16). A series of research and evaluative studies, including that by the government-funded National Foundation for Educational Research, have shown education for citizenship has failed to become embedded in schools since its inception. Although provision judged to be high quality was most often where citizenship was taught as a discrete subject, there remains a shortage of specialised citizenship teachers and schools were found to continue to regard citizenship as a cross-curricular theme and often merge delivery with that of PSHE. The low priority afforded to the subject and poor quality of teaching has reinforced staff and students' perceptions of the low value of citizenship. The Crick Report had fallen short of recommending citizenship to be delivered as a new and examined subject taught by specialist trained teachers, constraining the impact of these proposals in practice.

Perhaps of greater concern are the theoretical, as opposed to practical, flaws in the approach of the Crick Report. At a time when our world is becoming increasingly interdependent, the Report defined politics narrowly in terms of the nation state with the national prioritised over the global. Concerns as regards extremism in society have also been exacerbated in this period and these are illuminated by recent events. The failure of the Crick Report to meet the challenge of racism and discrimination head-on and to embed approaches for exploring the multiple identities of British citizens was once again exposed. It has been argued that other government policies have compounded these barriers to progress: for example, the resourcing of selective schools by the British government, including those according to religious belief, is said to be *not conducive to building effective networks of rights and responsibilities that stretch across cultural and social boundaries* (Faulks, 2006, page 72).

Recent developments in England

Significantly, in 2006 the government set up a review of diversity and citizenship curriculum to consider the teaching of ethnic, religious and cultural diversity across the entire school curriculum, up to the age of 19. The findings of the resultant Ajegbo Report (DfES, 2007) confirmed various weaknesses of the make-up and delivery of education for citizenship and proposed a new strand in the schools' citizenship curriculum, entitled 'Identity and Diversity: Living Together in the UK' that has since been adopted. Initial critiques of the Ajegbo Report suggest that the report's recommendations fail to reinforce the curriculum framework proposed by Crick (Osler, 2008).

While it is widely reported that teachers and schools in England are overburdened with constant policy change and multiple government initiatives, two recent acts of parliament have amplified and accelerated the responsibility of schools to make progress in their delivery of education for citizenship. The Race Relations (Amendment) Act 2000 requires schools to promote race equality. The Education and Inspections Act 2006 includes a statutory duty for schools to promote community cohesion which is now inspected by the Office of Standards in Education (OFSTED). Meanwhile, the debate surrounding education for citizenship in England's schools is complemented by a plethora of related government initiatives that make demands on schools to be sustainable or eco schools, promoting pupils' parliament and international schools awards, amongst other things.

Practical Task

The citizenship curriculum

In England the programme of study for each subject in the secondary curriculum is preceded by an *importance statement* that provides a rationale for the teaching of the subject. In 1998 the Advisory Group on Education for Citizenship and the Teaching of Democracy in Schools (part of the Qualifications and Curriculum Authority, QCA) identified three principles of effective citizenship education, that it should develop:

* social and moral responsibility;
* community involvement;
* political literacy.

The revised secondary curriculum introduced in schools in 2008 (QCA, 2008) aims to give schools greater flexibility to tailor learning to their learners' needs. It has three overarching aims, which incorporate the five outcomes of *Every Child Matters*. The aims are that the curriculum should enable all young people to become:

* successful learners who enjoy learning, make progress and achieve;
* confident individuals who are able to live safe, healthy and fulfilling lives;
* responsible citizens who make a positive contribution to society.

The new curriculum does recognise the importance of individual subjects but places increasing emphasis on the development of skills for life and work. There is less prescribed subject content in the new programmes of study. Read the programme of study for Citizenship at Key Stages 3 and 4, found at the Qualifications and Curriculum Authority (QCA) website (**http://curriculum.qca.org.uk/key-stages-3-and-4/subjects/citizenship/index.aspx**). Read it and consider the answers to these questions.

* In what ways are each of these three principles illustrated in the Citizenship Importance statement?
* Can you connect these three principles to the key concepts and processes that form the subsequent sections in the Citizenship programme of study?

Service-learning and America

(Case Study 2)

In America service-learning is one approach to citizenship education which integrates community service with the curriculum at all levels of education. The tradition of service-learning is grounded in theories of experiential education exemplified originally by community-based internships. The definition of service-learning (SL) is contested. For some, 'service to others' is the primary outcome while for others, this service is secondary to an 'academic strategy' which emphasises student learning. For each distinctive interpretation of the term, a variety of Service-Learning programmes exist from kindergarten through to higher education. Distinctions can be drawn between SL and work-based learning and 'pure' service activity or volunteering devoid of any focus on student learning.

What is clear is an emphasis on learning as opposed to teaching, drawing on theorists that propose that we learn through combinations of thought and action, reflection and practice, theory and application. Practitioners and researchers have become involved in this growing movement that cuts across individual subject areas and disciplines and would probably broadly agree on the following definition:

Service-Learning is a form of experiential education in which students engage in activities that address human and community needs together with structured opportunities intentionally designed to promote student learning and development. Reflection and reciprocity are key concepts of Service-Learning.

Jacoby, 1996, page 6

It has been acknowledged that the term 'service-learning' may restrict its influence and potential. The word 'service' itself has multiple interpretations dependent on context. There have been calls among service-learning advocates to look more carefully at concepts of civic engagement, political or community involvement (similar to those considered in the English citizenship curriculum) and education for citizenship recognising that a *new language is needed beyond service-learning to rally the troops and move the agenda forward* (Battistoni, 2006, page 15).

In America, college-student community service has a long history that includes the YMCA (Young Man's Christian Association) and Scout movement but came into public focus in the 1960s with President John F Kennedy's launch of the Peace Corps. The 1990s saw a significant increase in federal government support for service-learning, reflecting the support for communitarian approaches that cut across national party politics. The president championed the National and Community Service Trust Act in 1990, while three years later the next president outlined proposals for a new type of national service whereby credits for post-school national service could be used towards further education and training. More recently these federal initiatives have been consolidated in terms of compassionate conservatism.

There has been an increased emphasis in this time on the relationship between service-learning and citizenship. A particularly resilient initiative whose approach reflects this is National Campus Compact, an organisation of college and University presidents who promote public and community service that develops students' citizenship skills and helps campuses forge effective community partnerships. Twenty-one years after its launch, in 2006, it had over 1,000 campus members with the organisation claiming 298 million service hours completed by students on 25,000 different service learning programmes during 2005.

A growth of research into this emergent field has seen the International Conference of Service-Learning Research held annually in America since 2002. There has been substantial research into the pedagogical dimension as well as the evaluation of the learning outcomes for students of domestic service-learning and which include the following dimensions:

- *personal* – self-knowledge, spiritual growth, reward of helping others, more informed career choices, enhanced employability and changes in personal efficacy;
- *interpersonal* – working with others, leadership skills;
- *academic* – skills and links to further academic learning (life-long learning), critical thinking, problem solving, a greater engagement with discipline, more thoughtful approach to knowledge.

One of the leading research projects into Service-Learning in America (Eyler and Giles, 1999) found that *although policy makers and service-learning advocates promoted citizenship as a main goal of service-learning, students rarely think in those terms* (page 157). Its analysis of the learning outcomes found that Service-Learning contributes to the attainment of each element of a citizenship model that focuses on social responsibility and effective participation. This framework consists of Values (*'I ought to do'*), Knowledge (*'I know what I ought to do and why'*), Skills (*'I know how to do it'*), Efficacy (*'I can do it and it makes a difference'*) and Commitment (*'I must and will do'*). This responds to the challenge that SL has failed to look beyond a traditional charitable perspective to one grounded in the pursuit of social justice.

An area of particular relevance to this framework, within this and other contexts, is the link between learning and action and the forces that result in changes to behaviour. How do students move from increased awareness to action for change? For example, young people may acknowledge that they should dispose of litter themselves but in practice fail to do so. A greater emphasis on longitudinal studies is needed to examine actual citizenship behaviours over a period of time. It is also recognised that there has been considerably less attention paid to research into the impact of service-learning on the individuals and community organisations that are served.

Community action in Indian higher education

(Case Study 3)

In India the term 'social involvement' is preferred over 'service learning', although the two are very similar in philosophy and approach. An example of an Indian social involvement programme is one where undergraduate students are encouraged to learn through consistent and direct involvement with less privileged communities or groups than themselves through a variety of volunteering opportunities.

The core structure of the programme is:

- the sharing of knowledge and skills;
- the development of an inquiring mind;
- the analysis of socio-economic issues such as poverty, inequality and redistributive justice;
- the expression of a concern for the environment; and
- the realisation of one's own role in transforming the self and society.

The programme would be incomplete if it merely involved students in different social work activities without drawing out their thoughts and ideas triggered off through such engagement. It is this analysis of socio-economic issues, exploration of social justice and the realisation of their own social responsibility which is key.

Reflective Task

Citizenship in India

Read the following piece written by an Indian academic and director of an undergraduate social involvement programme:

Writers and thinkers on economic and business matters seem to be rocking to the beat of India's booming economy. The reasons for their hype and excitement are many – the GDP is growing at a healthy rate, the sensex (Bombay Stock Exchange Sensitive Index) is soaring, upper class incomes are expanding and shopping malls are multiplying. They seem to be cheered by the surge in computers and information technology which could help people stay connected 24:7 with the developed world and yet remain disconnected from the real India.

We have no intention of spoiling the party but, unmasked, India's performance on the world stage could look dull and depressing. For example this is a land which consistently attains the top rank for:

- *the most malnourished people;*
- *the largest number of TB cases and deaths;*
- *the highest number of people living in absolute poverty;*
- *the huge number of children not in school.*

UNHDP, 2008

The primary thought that every educated Indian should grapple with is: why are so many Indians unable to read and write?

Almost all countries in the developed world and in Asia, which have transformed their economies, have done so by investing in elementary education. Their governments have ensured that the people have the ability to read, write and interact in a way that enables their participation in a modern economy. In India, the poor quality of basic education has limited the sphere of economic expansion. Educational inequality is one of the main reasons for income inequality. We have to tackle this situation. Therefore, the majority of our students are involved in teaching children who study in needy schools.

D'Costa, 2008

- How do you think this academic would describe the concept of citizenship?
- Why is it so important to her for students to engage in social involvement programmes as a means of citizenship education?
- What sort of opportunities might she plan for her students?

Students are expected to maintain a daily record of their activities, observations and experiences. They then identify similarities and disparities between the observed realities and the officially stated government version. They then work on projects trying to relate their experiences to established theories, and social, economic or political trends. This, it is argued, helps to deepen their understanding of the situations and the people they encounter, in their immediate and broader community and their place in this as active citizens (Bamber *et al.*, 2009).

This example from India is not on the scale of the other two case studies, but it is significant as an example of a small citizenship initiative, of which there are many other examples worldwide. Of course, it is impossible to make any definite claims about the extent of the benefits. However, early research does suggest that it has resulted in many students becoming more informed, mature and conscious of their responsibilities as citizens of India (Bamber *et al.*, 2009).

Reflective Task

Concepts of citizenship and places of education

The student survey in the IEA Civic Education Study in 1999, referred to earlier, examined young people's attitudes towards citizenship. Participants were asked to rate on a scale of 1 to 4 how important they felt a number of indicators of citizenship were for explaining what a good adult citizen is or what a good adult citizen does. This revealed young people's conceptions of citizenship. The survey was designed so that some of these items reflected elements of 'conventional' citizenship (such as voting in an election) and others 'social-movement'-related citizenship (such as taking part in activities to protect the environment).

Indicators of conventional citizenship:

- joining a political party;
- knowing about a country's history;
- following political issues in the newspaper, or on radio or on TV;
- showing respect for government representatives (leaders, officials);
- engaging in political discussions.

Indicators of social-movement-related citizenship:

- participating in activities to benefit people in the community (society);
- participating in a peaceful protest against a law believed to be unjust;
- taking part in activities promoting human rights.

Reflecting on the above indicators, consider these questions:

- Consider your own understanding of what it means to be a citizen.
- As a group discuss the aspects of citizenship illuminated by the case studies in this chapter. What indicators of citizenship are not included here that you think would be worthwhile to investigate young people's attitudes towards? How might you go about this?
- How do your own experiences of citizenship education, as a pupil or student, compare to those in this chapter?

Education for global citizenship

The development of globalisation has promoted discussions about global interdependence across a range of disciplines. This is no less the case within citizenship education, or indeed comparative education. The idea that people can simultaneously have multiple identities and attachments was promoted by Nussbaum. She describes a *world citizen* (1996) as someone who confesses an interest in and acts upon concerns for both distant strangers as well as next-door neighbours. Citizenship education concerned only with one's own country is clearly insufficient for our global world.

Multiple understandings of global citizenship have developed in public and academic debate. In the media, the term is sometimes used to describe a loose sense of belonging and responsibility to a global community and is demonstrated by acts of charity and the development of intercultural skills. Schattle (2006) has suggested there are two overarching views of global citizenship. Firstly, a civic republican view that emphasises concepts such as awareness, responsibility, participation and cultural empathy, and secondly, a libertarian view that emphasises international mobility and competitiveness. Simplistically the former may be represented by the global activist who stands up for their beliefs on the local or global stage and the latter by someone with the skills and values to compete in the global marketplace who may be disengaged from any political participation.

Oxfam is one of a number of international NGOs that promote education for global citizenship. It characterises the Global Citizen as someone who:

- is aware of the wider world and has a sense of their own role as a world citizen;
- respects and values diversity;
- has an understanding of how the world works;
- is outraged by social injustice;
- participates in the community at a range of levels, from the local to the global;
- is willing to act to make the world a more equitable and sustainable place;
- takes responsibility for their actions (Oxfam, 2006).

Oxfam outlines the subject content, skills, values and attitudes that it believes enable young people to develop a critical understanding of global issues and engage in action for change. Resources based on key concepts such as values and perceptions, diversity, conflict resolution, social justice and sustainable development have been created to help teachers in the UK address the cross-curricular theme of the 'Global Dimension' (DfES, 2005). Oxfam endorses active learning strategies that challenge the values and attitudes of both students and teachers: a maximal approach that goes beyond learning about other people and other places. A popular strategy has been to encourage young people to communicate with communities outside of their own country. The transformation of transport, media, technology and communication systems has provided youngsters, particularly from the North (developed world), with countless opportunities to interact, often face to face, with citizens of nations across the world.

International Service-Learning (ISL) presents a significant opportunity for students to undertake volunteering experiences overseas that changes the way they view the world. There still exists only limited research on the impact of ISL on student learning and development. This remains largely anecdotal, covering a range of learning from intercultural competence, language skills, personal development and skills of self-reliance to a deeper understanding of global problems related to their academic study. There has been a proliferation of organisations offering young people from the North (developed world) volunteering opportunities in resource-poor communities in the South (developing world). Inevitably this has led to organisations, including institutions of higher education, operating without reflection on their impact and the experience they offer young people.

Research has shown that ISL students who envision a commitment to act upon their transformed view of the world struggle to translate their critical awareness into meaningful action. Scholars have also noted a recent phenomenon whereby individuals may bypass a sense of responsibility within their own local and national communities to take action on the global stage.

It is insufficient, however, to feel and express a sense of solidarity with others elsewhere if we cannot establish a sense of solidarity with others in our own communities, especially those others whom we perceive to be different from ourselves.

Osler and Starkey, 2005, page 93

Global citizenship advocates in the North have been criticised for promoting global citizenship as a minority world initiative: excluding members of less developed nations whose voice is less easily heard on the world stage. A grassroots movement that has challenged this perspective is the Global Campaign for Education, founded in 1999. This international coalition, based in

South Africa, brings together Civil Society organisations, NGOs, teacher unions and child rights activists to promote 'Education for All'. A week-long initiative in 2008 saw 8.8 million young people from over 100 countries take part in the world's biggest lesson to raise awareness of the value of education.

It would be expected that education for global citizenship promotes a set of skills and ideals that translate across borders. Studies have in fact shown varied constructions of education for global citizenship. For example, the Oxfam approach reflects certain universal principles, yet does not include an explicit human rights framework. Similarly, the capacity to influence political decision making at various levels would seem to be a key plank of any education for global citizenship. Although political literacy forms one of the key strands of citizenship education in England, this does not feature in the Oxfam guidance for promoting responsible global citizenship. Furthermore, Andreotti (2006) draws on post-colonial theory to distinguish between 'soft' and 'critical' global citizenship education. The former perpetuates existing power relations between countries and individuals around the world and the latter challenges the learner to interpret global interdependence in new ways and envision a transformed relationship between the North and the South.

Practical Task

Young people and their readiness for citizenship

The 1999 IEA study, referred to earlier, has been followed up with a new study, the International Civic and Citizenship Education Study. This will investigate, in a range of countries, the ways in which young people are prepared and consequently ready and able to undertake their roles as citizens. The study uses an assessment framework (IEA, 2007) that is organised into three dimensions: content, affective-behavioural and cognitive. The first dimension will see researchers assess young people's understanding of the subject matter associated with civics and citizenship, the second dimension to measure their involvement in citizenship-related activities (such as volunteering) and their attitude towards citizenship-related concepts and the third dimension to assess the thinking processes involved, such as reasoning and analysing.

Write a list of questions you could ask young people in your own country to investigate the way they are prepared and consequently ready to undertake their role as citizens, either locally or globally. Which of the three dimensions (content, affective-behavioural and cognitive) do the questions investigate?

Have a look at some of the questions used in the 1999 study, available on the internet at **www.terpconnect.umd.edu/~jtpurta/**, to get you started.

Chapter Summary

This chapter has discussed citizenship education and identified some problems in constructing a curriculum or approach to education for global citizenship.

- In recent years there has been a growing interest in citizenship education.
- In some countries, such as England, traditions of 'Global Education' and 'Citizenship Education' have evolved alongside each other.

- This division between global education and citizenship education may perpetuate a less relevant understanding of citizenship and a deficient view of global education.
- With increased globalisation it is no longer sufficient to consider citizenship with regard to your nation state only.
- Some academics and practitioners consider active participation as a key element in citizenship education.
- Forms of education, illustrated by the case studies and approaches discussed in this chapter, should be brought together under the banner of global citizenship education.

Research focus

Task 1

An interesting read to help you further your understanding of citizenship education and global citizenship is:

- Davies, I (2002) Education for a better world, in Davies, I, Gregory, I and McGuinn, N (eds) *Key debates in education*. London: Continuum, 113–130.

Davies, in his chapter, debates some of the issues and dilemmas in educating people for a better world and makes particular reference to citizenship in this pursuit. McGuinn, a co-author of the book, then responds to Davies' thinking, looking particularly at the role of the teacher in developing global citizens. Read the chapter, paying particular attention to the issues Davies raises. After reading McGuinn's response, outline what you understand to be the main differences between Davies' and McGuinn's arguments.

Task 2

In the following article Davies and Reid present an argument for introducing global citizenship education that brings together citizenship education and global education.

- Davies, I and Reid, A (2005) Globalising citizenship education? A critique of 'global education' and 'citizenship education'. *British Journal of Educational Studies* 53, 1: 66–89.

Read this article and consider it in relation to the case studies and content of this chapter. What do you consider to be the rationale for adopting the approach favoured by Davies and Reid? Make notes identifying the teaching and learning strategies that may be drawn upon to make this vision a reality.

What arguments are there for not merging citizenship with global education?

References

Andreotti, V (2006) Soft versus critical global citizenship education. *Policy and Practice* 3. Belfast: Centre for Global Education.

Bamber, P, Bignold, W and D'Costa, C (2009) 'The impact of social involvement and community engagement on students in higher education in India and the UK', Journal of the World Universities Forum. 2.

Battistoni, R (2006) Approaching democratic engagement: Research findings on civic learning and civic practice, in Billig, S (ed.) *Service-learning: Research to transform the field*. Greenwich, CN: Information Age Publishing, 3–16.

Davies, I (2002) Education for a better world in Davies, I, Gregory, I and McGuinn, N (eds) *Key debates in education*. London: Continuum, 113–130.

Davies, I and Reid, A (2005) Globalising citizenship education? A critique of 'global education' and 'citizenship education'. *British Journal of Educational Studies* 53, 1: 66–89.

D'Costa, C (2008) Interview of D'Costa, C, by Bamber, P. St Xavier's College, Mumbai, India, 21 July 2008. Unpublished interview.

Department for Education and Skills [DfES] (2005) *Developing the global dimension in the school curriculum*. Glasgow: DfID.

Department for Education and Skills [DfES] (2007) *Diversity and citizenship curriculum review.* London: DfES.

Eyler, J and Giles, DE (1999). *Where's the learning in service-learning?* San Francisco, CA: Jossey-Bass.

Faulks, K (2006) Education for citizenship in England's secondary schools: A critique of current principle and practice. *Journal of Education Policy* 21, 1: 59–74.

Heater, D (1990) *Citizenship: The civic ideal in world history, politics and education.* London: Longman.

IEA (2007) *International civic and citizenship education study assessment framework.* Amsterdam: IEA.

Jacoby, B (1996) *Service-Learning and higher education: Concepts and practices.* San Francisco, CA: Jossey-Bass.

Jochum, V, Pratten, B and Wilding, K (2005) *Civil renewal and active citizenship: A guide to the debate.* Available at: **www.ncvo-vol.org.uk/publications/publication.asp?id=1512** (accessed 8 May 2009).

Kerr, D and Nelson, J (2006) *International review of curriculum and assessment frameworks. Active citizenship in INCA countries: definitions, policies, practices and outcomes.* Final report. Available at: **www.inca.org.uk/pdf/Active_Citizenship_Report.pdf** (accessed 8 May 2009).

Nussbaum, M (1996) *For love of country: Debating the limits of patriotism.* Boston, MA: Beacon Press.

Osler, A (2008) Citizenship education and the Ajegbo report: Re-imagining a cosmopolitan nation. *London Review of Education* 6, 1: 11–25.

Osler, A and Starkey, H (2005) *Changing citizenship: Democracy and inclusion in education.* Berkshire: Open University Press.

Oxfam (2006) *Education for global citizenship: A guide for schools*. Available at: **www.oxfam.org.uk/education/gc/files/education_for_global_citizenship_a_guide_for_schools.pdf** (accessed 8 May 2009).

Qualifications and Curriculum Authority (QCA) (1998) *Education for citizenship and teaching of democracy in schools (Crick Report).* London: QCA.

Qualifications and Curriculum Authority (QCA) (2008) *The new secondary curriculum.* Available at: **www.curriculum.qca.org.uk/** (accessed 8 May 2009).

Schattle, H (2006) Communicating global citizenship: Multiple discourses beyond the academy. *Citizenship Studies* 9, 2: 119–133.

Index

absenteeism 53
accountability 5
accuracy of research 14
active citizenship 111
administrative practices 5
affirmative action practices 71
Ajegbo Report 114
Ancient Greeks and Romans 7
anti-social behaviour 113
arithmetic teaching in France 9
Arnold, Matthew 7, 9
Assessment for Learning (AFL) 42
Assessment of Learning (AOL) 42

Bachelor of Education (B. Ed.) 80
'belonging', sense of 5
bias 14
Birth to Three Matters 25
Bologna Agreement 76
brain development 22
Bruner 36
Butler Act (1944) 34, 53

Callaghan, James 82
Cambridge Primary Review 37
Carr, Margaret 28
Ceausescu, Nicolae 32, 101, 103
Centre for Educational Research and
    Innovation (CERI) 10
Certificate in Education (Cert Ed) 80, 81
Childcare Strategy for England 27
childminder 27
Children Act (1989) (UK) 24, 101, 103
Children Act (2004) (UK) 34, 54, 101, 102, 103
children at risk 5
Children's Centres 18, 27, 105
Children's Commissioners 95
children's rights 8, 29
Children's Rights law (2004) (Romania) 103
Children's Society 108
Children's Workforce Development Council 27
China 7; education for citizenship 110;
    government influence on universities 67–8;
    higher education 70; higher education
    inspection 73; higher education research
    75; mature students 76; professionalisation
    of academics in 71; salaries of academics 73
citizenship education 83, 109–22
City Academies (CAs) 54
City Technology Colleges (CTCs) 54

civic engagement 115
civic republicanism 110
classroom assistants 85
Climbié, Victoria 84, 101
Common Assessment Framework 102
communitarianism 110
community-based internships 115
community colleges 71
Community Schools 53
comparative teacher education 90–1
comprehensive schools 7
Comte, Auguste 57
Connexions Service 105
continuing professional development (CPD) 80
corporal punishment 8
cost effectiveness 5
Council for Accreditation of Teacher Education
    (CATE) 86–7
Crick Report 113, 114
cultural identity 5
cultural relativism 96–7
culture shock 5
curriculum 5; change 5, 8, 83–7; Early Years
    25–6; International Baccalaureate 8;
    national core curriculum (NCC) 56, 57;
    see also National Curriculum; primary
    curriculum
Curriculum for Excellence 25
Curriculum Guidance for the Foundation Stage
    25

Davies, Rose 30
day care 18
day nurseries 18
Dearing Report (1997) 64, 66, 71, 73
decentralisation 5
definition of comparative education 4–5
denominational (faith) schools 41, 53
Department for Children, Schools and Families
    (DCSF) 10, 34, 38, 54
Department for Education and Science (DfES)
    85
Department for Education and Skills (DfES) 10
Department for Innovation, Universities and
    Skills (DIUS) 10
Department for International Development
    (DfID) 14
Didactic Triangle 11, 12–14
Directorate-General for Education and Culture
    (EC) 90

distrust of other cultures 5
Durkheim, Emile 57

Early Learning Goals 28
Early Years curriculum 25–6
Early Years Foundation Stage (EYFS) 25, 28, 37
Early Years Professional (EYP) 27
'economic migrants' 111
Education (Butler) Act (1944) 34, 53
Education and Inspections Act (2006) 114
'Education for Mutual Understanding' 84
Education Guardian 58
Education Reform Act (1988) 24, 34, 113
Education Welfare Act (2000) 41
educational psychologists 27
Educational Testing Service (USA) 50
Effective Provision for Pre School Education
    (EPPE) 22, 23, 27
Elementary Education Act (1870) 33, 81
Eleven Plus 53
England: academic salaries 72; challenges to
    integration 105; citizenship education
    113–14; recent developments in 114;
    research 75; school (5–16) 96; science in
    57; welfare 99–100
Enriched Curriculum project (Northern Ireland)
    25
equality of opportunity 5
ethnocentrism 96–7
European Commission (EU) 48, 90
European Court of Human Rights 8
European Union 32
Every Child Matters (ECM) 19, 24, 34, 54, 84,
    101–2, 105
Excellence in Schools 113
exchange programmes 15
Extended Schools 105

faith schools 41, 53
fear of other cultures 5
Finland 7; science in 58
Finnish National Board of Education (FNBE)
    56
Forster Act (1870) 33, 81
Foundation Phase (Wales) 25
Foundation Schools, 53
Foundation Stage 36, 44
Framework for Children's Learning in the
    Foundation Phase (Wales) 25
France, arithmetic teaching in 9
Froebel, Friedrich 19, 22, 23
functional theory 57
funding 65–8, 74–5

gap years 15
GCE Advanced (A) levels 55
General Certificate of Secondary Education
    (GCSE) 55

General Teaching Council (GTC) 87
generality–specificity trap 15
Germany, higher education research 75
Global Campaign for Education 120
Global Citizen 120
global citizenship 119–21
globalisation 4, 15
graduate jobs75
'graduate tax' approach 66
grammar schools 7, 53

Haddow Report (1926) 34
Higher Education Funding Council for Wales
    65
Higher Education Funding Council of England
    65
higher education, purpose of 74–5
hostility towards other cultures 5

'Identity and Diversity: Living Together in the
    UK' 114
Ideological Cross 11–12
inclusion 5, 26
Independent Review of the Primary
    Curriculum 38
independent schools 7
India: community action in 1higher education
    17–18; education in 69–70; government
    influence on universities 67; government
    inspection 73; higher education fees in 75;
    higher education research 75;
    professionalization of academics in 71;
    salaries of academics 72–3
initial teacher education and training 80
insider research 7
Institute for Learning and Teaching in Higher
    Education (ILT) 71
Institute of Education Science 9
intelligentsia 8
International Association for the Evaluation of
    Educational Achievement (IAE) 48, 49, 50;
    Civic Education Study (IEA CIVED study)
    111
International Baccalaureate 8, 54
International Civic and Citizenship Education
    Study 121
International Conference of Service-Learning
    Research 115
International Service-Learning (ISL) 120
International Year of the Child (1979) 29
interpretivist model 6
Ireland: education 32; primary education
    in 41–2; Primary School Curriculum
    41; statutory age of schooling 32,
    44–5
Irish-speaking schools (Gaelscoileanna) 41

Japan 7

Kennedy, John F. 115
Key Stages 36, 44, 53, 55, 114
kindergarten 18, 44
knowledge societies 25
Korea 7

Laming, Lord 84
league tables 9, 34, 49
'Learning and Teaching Scotland' 84
learning mentors 85
Learning Stories 28
liberalism 110
literacy 7–8, 34, 49
local authorities (LAs) 54

McMillan, Rachel 19
McMillan, Margaret 19, 27
Montessori, Maria 19–20, 22, 23
multi-denominational (mixed-faith) schools; 41
multiculturalism 5
Mussolini, Benito 20

National and Community Service Trust Act
    (1990) (USA) 115
National Campus Compact 115
National Centre for Education Statistics 50
national core curriculum (NCC) 56, 57
National Council for Curriculum and
    Assessment (NCCA) 42, 43
National Curriculum 5, 34, 36, 37, 54–5, 83
National Curriculum Authority 73
National Foundation for Educational Research
    114
National Institute of Technology (India) 75
National Standards for Under 8s Day Care and
    Childminding 25
Netherlands: higher education research 75
New Zealand: Strategic Plan for Early
    Childhood Education 28
non-State-aided private primary schools 41
Northern Ireland 8; curriculum 84
numeracy 7–8, 34
nurseries 18, 44

Office for Standards in Education (OFSTED)
    34, 54, 86, 114
Organisation for Economic Co-operation and
    Development (OECD) 10, 18, 48, 51, 58
Owen, Robert 19
Oxfam 120

parents, partnership with 23, 24
Parsons 57
Peace Corps. 115
pedagogical research 8
pedagogista (early years' practitioner) 27
Peers Early Education Partnership intervention
    programme 23

Pestalozzi 19, 20, 22
Piaget, Jean 36
Plato 7
playgroups 18
Plowden Report 24
Poland: educational reform in the 1700s 7;
    government influence on teacher education
    in 90; National Curriculum 88; teacher
    education in 87–90
Polish State Accreditation Committee 90
political apathy 113
Polo, Marco 7
postgraduate certificates in education (PGCE)
    80
poverty 48, 105–6
primary curriculum: in England 36–8; in
    Ireland 41–2; in Romania 39–40
primary education: England 33–6
private school 14
professionalisation of academic staff 71–3
Progettazione 26
Programme for International Student
    Assessment (PISA) 10, 14, 48, 51–3, 58–9,
    60
Progress International Reading Literacy Study
    (PIRLS) 9, 48
PSHE 114
Public Education Bill (1820) 33
public schools 81
Pupil Referral Units (PRUs) 54

Qualifications and Curriculum Authority (QCA)
    37, 54
qualified teacher status (QTS) 27, 54, 55, 85
Quality Assurance Agency (QAA) 73
quality assurance and standards of higher
    education 73–4
quantitative methods of research 9
questionnaires 9

Race Relations (Amendment) Act 2000 114
Reggio Emilia 20, 24, 26, 27, 28, 29
research contracts, HE 74–5
rights of the child 8, 29
Robbins Report 80
Romania 32, 95; challenges to integration in
    105–6; National Curriculum 39; primary
    education in 38–40; Rural Education Project
    39; statutory age of schooling 44
Rose, Sir Jim 38
Rousseau, Jean-Jacques 7

salaries, academic 72–3
School Admissions Code 53
school leaving age, England 34
school-centred initial teacher training (SCITTs)
    84
science 57

Scotland 8; academic salaries 72; curriculum 84; fees 65; senior secondary and junior secondary schools 7
Scottish Consultative Council on the Curriculum 84
Scottish Higher Education Funding Council 65
Scottish Parliament 24, 84
Scottish Schools (Parental Involvement) Act (2006) 24
Scout movement 115
secondary education: in England 53–5; in Finland 55–7
secondary modern schools 7, 53
secondary technical schools 53
service-learning (SL) 115–17
Siraj-Blatchford, Iram 30
Skinner 36
social care and education: in England 101–2; in Romania 103–4
social care policies: in England 99–100; in Romania100–1
social change 104–5
social construction of childhood 97–9
'social involvement' 117
'social justice' 68, 69
social policy 104–5
social workers 27
South Africa: citizenship education 110
Spartan education 7
Special Educational Needs and Disability Act 2001 55
Special Schools 41, 54
Specialist Schools 54
speech therapists 27
'spider's web' model 28
Start Right report (1994) 24
Statistics Canada 50
statutory ages of schooling 32, 44–5
Statutory Assessment Tests (SATs) 34, 36, 42
Steiner, Rudolph 19, 20, 22
'step' model 28
streaming 53
student employment, USA 76
student fees, UK 65, 75
'student loans' 66
study abroad 15, 76
subjective knowledge 7
Supporting Assessment in Primary School 42
Sure Start 23, 24
sustained shared thinking 27
Sweden 7

Te Whariki 15, 21, 24, 28, 29
teacher autonomy 5
Teacher Development Agency 65
teacher education 80–92
Teacher Training Agency (TTA) 83, 87
Teaching and Higher Education Act (1998) 87

teaching qualifications 71, 80
technical schools 7
Thatcher, Margaret 83
Training and Development Agency for Schools (TDA) 87
travellers' tales 7
Trends in International Mathematics and Science Study (TIMSS) 9, 14, 48, 50, 52, 53, 57, 60
tripartite structure 7
Trust School 53

United Nations Children's Fund see United Nations International Children's Emergency Fund
United Nations Committee on the Rights of the Child 95, 97, 104
United Nations Convention on the Rights of the Child (UNCRC) 29, 94, 95–6, 97, 101, 106
United Nations: definition of a child 97
United Nations Development Programme 50
United Nations Education, Scientific and Cultural Organisation (UNESCO) 9, 25; Centre for Comparative Education Research (UCCER) 10; Institute for National Statistics 10
United Nations General Assembly 29
United Nations International Children's Emergency Fund (UNICEF) 21, 95–6, 101
universities, UK, government influence 67
University Grant Commission (UGC) 66, 73
USA 7; Department of Education 50; Department of Education National Centre for Education Statistics 9; funding for higher education 67; government influence on universities 68; higher education 70–1; higher education research 75; professionalism 71; quality of higher education 73–4; remuneration for academics 73; service-learning 115–17; students categories 76

'value for money' 21
values 6
Voluntary Aided Schools 53, 54
Voluntary Controlled Schools 54
Vygotsky, Leo 26, 36

Wales: academic salaries 72; Curriculum Cymreig. 84; research 75; top-up fees 65
'welfare' in England 99–100
World Bank 50
world citizen 119
World War I 7
World War II 100

Young Man's Christian Association (YMCA) 116